"Renewal of our human int W9-COY-950 the deepest imperative of our times. The Earth we see about us is the only Earth we have. Wayne Simsic's book guides us into a renewal of our primordial intimacy with Earth both by accounts of his own experience and by recovering for us some of the more remarkable passages of our past literature that assist in this renewal."

Thomas Berry
Author, *Befriending the Earth*

"Wayne Simsic has written one of the few books that addresses the question, 'Just what does nature inspire us to?' Chapter by chapter, he explores some of the intuitions and feelings that are awakened by contact with nature."

Chris Laning
EarthLight Magazine

"Even the millions who can experience only vicariously the luxury of retreat into the solitude of a forest can find inspiration in this book."

Sr. Vernard Nichaus
Sisters Today

"If you encounter God in nature—or want to—this is your book. Simsic sings of a sacarmental universe in the tradition of Celtic piety."

Jim Scully
The Pecos Benedictine

"Here are wonder-filled meditations upon nature in a variety of settings to proclaim the mystery and beauty of God's creation and our reverential response to it."

Values and Visions

"This book is an invitation to encounter God in nature. Simsic weaves together his own experiences at Little Salmon Creek and on a lake in Canada with the insights of mystics, poets, artists, and naturalists. The effect is powerful and evocative. The reader is drawn out of his or her armchair and into nature. There, Simsic suggests, one can find God and oneself."

J. Milburn Thompson
Emmanuel Magazine

"Everyone should read this book. All of us can be re-awakened to see Earth as sacred. It shows us the beauty of our Earth and how we are to reverence it. Simsic brings out how even the destructive forces in nature are glorious."

Gilbert Padilla, Pastor
Author, *Refreshment in the Desert*

"Wayne Simsic makes it plain that nature is the teacher of prayer and the dwelling place of divine mystery. He summons us to a deeply incarnational form of prayer, full of wonder, gratitude, and celebration. A most rewarding book!"

Charles Cummings, O.C.S.O.
Author, *Eco-Spirituality: Toward a Reverent Life*

"In nature we can wonder at the awesome and unfathomable work of our Creator. Our lives become caught up in the daily routine of work. We lose the ability to wonder and appreciate creation; therefore, how can we pray? Simsic's book shows the way."

Prairie Messenger

"Simsic is not trying to persuade us to ignore the transcendence of God, but he is challenging us to remember the immanence of God and to use it well for our spiritual growth and development."

St. Anthony Messenger

Songs of Sunrise
Seeds of Prayer

WAYNE SIMSIC

TWENTY-THIRD PUBLICATIONS
Mystic, CT 06355

This book was originally published in 1991 under the title of *Natural Prayer: Encountering God in Nature.*

Twenty-Third Publications
P.O. Box 180
185 Willow Street
Mystic, CT 06355
(203) 536-2611
800-321-0411

ISBN 0-89622-448-1
Library of Congress Catalog Card Number 90-71659

Preface

I wish, O Son of the living God, O ancient, eternal King,

For a hidden little hut in the wilderness that it may be my dwelling.

An all-grey little lake to be by its side.

A clear pool to wash away sins through the grace of the Holy Spirit.

Quite near, a beautiful wood around it on every side.

To nurse many-voiced birds, hiding it with its shelter.

A southern aspect for warmth, a little brook across its floor,

A choice land with many gracious gifts such as be good for every plant.

Raiment and food enough for me from the King of fair fame, And I to be sitting for a while praying God in every place.

"The Hermit's Song"   (Celtic Prayer)

While swimming in the ocean, hiking in the mountains, or following a forest path we find such beauty and pleasure in the natural world that we feel the quality of our lives change and we sense a deeper harmony with Mystery. We experience a unity with a sacred dimension without being able to explain it; we can only rejoice. A prayer fills our hearts and we feel alive, vulnerable, and receptive to the depths of nature and to the depths of our very being. The prayer that emerges is like the prayer of the Celtic hermit who sings of a desire for clear pools of water, sheltering forests, melodic bird song, and gifts from Earth and King so that he can spend his days praising God.

The hermit may have been an ascetic but his asceticism did not make him hostile toward nature; rather, it purified his vision and allowed him to see a sacramental universe where birds, streams, and natural phenomena were signs of God's grace.

In the tradition of Celtic spirituality, hermits, scribes, and anchorites abandoned themselves to spiritual work and at the same time cultivated a passion for seas, mountains, and wild creatures. Their prayers reveal a power of soul that could only come from being rooted in both spirit and Earth. Our need to regain a prayer that is linked to Earth has become a vital issue today. We find ourselves yearning for a deeper relationship with nature, one that goes beyond the superficial and has relevancy for our spiritual lives. We sense that without a relationship with nature our souls may very well remain hidden from us and we may lose participation in the wholeness and holiness of life.

Our ecological difficulties have forced us to recognize that there is something missing in our spirituality itself. We need a more creative, prayerful relationship with the natural world. We may be realizing, more than ever before, that the soul itself corresponds to the deepest meaning of the universe.

This book describes a prayer that moves beyond the surface of the natural world and penetrates to the heart of physical reality, a reality which is not empty of power and sacredness but is dynamic and holy. It describes an incarnational prayer that embraces the world in its fullness, in the belief that it is through Christ that all creation exists. It is a prayer that finds intimacy with nature only through humility, reverence, and sacrifice. The word "prayer" here can mean specific prayers but it also includes our whole life in our longing for God's love and the relationships that intensify this longing. Prayer encompasses all beings—humans, animals, plants, elements—in our journey to God.

Although this book draws on many resources, it originated primarily in my own awakening to the intimate relationship between nature and prayer that occurred during periods of solitude in the Allegheny Mountains of Pennsylvania. It was here, along Little Salmon Creek, that I began to realize how dramatically the environment can affect prayer. Little Salmon Creek itself had a potent role to play in all of this, since creeks have gurgled through my memory since childhood and have become part of my mind and heart as much as rivers and oceans. I have found mysteries floating in the riffles of this creek and, listening to her song, discovered a passageway into nature and into my own consciousness. I learned a prayer along this creek that was sometimes difficult but more often joyous and praise-filled.

Chapters 1 and 2, then, describe the power of nature, whether in the form of creeks, rivers, or oceans, to pull us outward and draw us toward the mystery and beauty of God. This is a difficult prayer for some to imagine, for we have inherited a prayer that is more inward and individualistic, emphasizing withdrawal from nature in order to find God. As a result, we must recall what it means to turn outward and discover a path of prayer through the natural world.

Chapters 3 and 4 explore the responses of wonder and reverence that occur when we enter the depths of nature and begin to understand how intimately nature is related to our own spiritual lives. Both wonder and reverence are an essential prelude for any prayer that will celebrate the gift of existence.

Chapters 5 and 6 describe a prayer that evolves from an encounter with the womb of silence at the heart of the natural world, and a vision of divine light that pours through all beings and is their origin and their life. The experience of silence makes us aware of the fire that is God's silence. The vision of light introduces us to the mark of divinity that is in all things and that binds us to them. Awakening to both the silence and light, we hunger to find the holy everywhere in the world.

The last chapter is a celebration of praise in response to the divine incarnate in nature and in our own hearts. It is through praise that we discover that all nature, if we have ears to hear, cries out with its own praise. We are not alone in our praise, but we include the celebration that is already resonating throughout Earth, the music at the heart of physical reality.

Dedication

For my mother, Susan,
who has given so much of her life
to the care of others,
and whose love for gardens
and wild roses
brought me home to Earth.

Acknowledgments

Many people have left their imprint on this manuscript during its development, reading it and offering valuable comments and support, and encouraging my efforts to find solitude in nature. In particular, I want to thank Bill and Diane Kelly, John and Diane Barrett, Sr. Margaret Mach, V.S.C., Mil and Bic Thompson, Bob Grgic, Laura Urgo, and especially Sr. Mercia Madigan, O.S.U., who continually encouraged me when words and inspiration failed.

My family—my Mother to whom this book is lovingly dedicated, Craig, Mary, Joe, Frank, and particularly Sue and Ed—supplied a great deal of support and enthusiasm. They have grounded my life and my work in more ways than I can say.

I am most grateful to two scholars. Professor William Cook of Geneseo University in New York introduced me to the Franciscan perspective toward nature in a dramatic way during a National Endowment for the Humanities seminar he directed in Italy. Professor Ewert Cousins, a renowned Franciscan scholar, disclosed the possibilities of nature mysticism during a National Endowment for the Humanities seminar on mysticism he directed at Fordham University. Both of these men are not only highly regarded academicians but inspirational teachers who influenced my thinking on nature significantly.

I owe a special debt to the faculty, staff, and students of Lake Catholic High School in Mentor, Ohio, who for many years reinforced my work and my interest in nature.

Finally, there have been many companions through the years who have shared their solitude as well as their insights and appreciation for the natural world. I am deeply appreciative to all of them, and they, no doubt, will find their influence represented in these pages.

Some portions of this book appeared earlier in *Spiritual Life*, *Living Prayer*, and *Sisters Today*.

Contents

At the Side
of Little Salmon Creek

And all the waters
Of all the streams
Sang in my veins
That summer day.
Theodore Roethke, "The Waking"

There are places in nature that attract our attention because of their magic and power. They can make the blood rush and the consciousness expand—they are places that we do not so much choose but feel drawn to in order to work out, in some inexplicable way, the meaning of our lives. Eventually, the place itself becomes sacred, alive with the stories of our spiritual adventure, and we know we have found a home for the soul.

I discovered a place like this in the Allegheny Forest. To get there you drive a steep, gutted, logging road into a valley which, no matter how many times I enter it, seems lost and hidden. The mountains flanking the valley hover around a white slip of water, Little Salmon Creek. Standing on the logging road and looking down the slope of a hill you can see the creek in various places emerging from the forest interior long enough to catch the sun in its froth before it disappears into the dark foliage. The banks bend and contort in an erratic dance as they make their way into the thick of the forest.

Thomas Merton says somewhere that when a solitary inhabits a particular place for a time the place itself becomes one with the solitude. This place along Little Salmon Creek has woven itself into my prayer and solitude. The light and shadow of the forest have become the light and shadow of my heart. This was a surprising feeling for someone who expected to find only peace and quiet. The forest engaged my heart and the result was drama; even the limitations of being in one place did not restrict the drama. Returning again and again, in and out of season, I felt like a hermit who returns to a cave knowing that the cave itself will teach solitude.

Sitting beside the creek this afternoon, I allow the motion of the water to capture my attention and lure my mind into lazy swirls and long sloping curls. My eyes drift with the water's changing pattern and are lulled by the slow rhythm. I am lost in the sweep of a small wave or the twirling of a floating leaf—my consciousness so absorbed that it flows along the bank with ease, discovering a way into the dark stillness of my being.

Nothing much happens along the side of creeks but maybe this is the reason they are able to drift into our hearts and minds and suggest something more. Remember the creeks of childhood? They pulled us along their banks to wider worlds promising innocence and mystery. They taught the rise and fall of Earth and captured the imagination, bearing us away in a liquid babble. The creeks of childhood were shallow, but mysteries swirled over their rocky bottoms.

I sit beside Little Salmon Creek and lose myself in the dazzling sunlight leaping on the water. I follow its winding bank because it offers a path into the mountains and into the sifting sediment of my own spiritual life. This creek has become so much a part of my consciousness that it has begun to reflect the longing that courses through my veins. When I leave it I find its song ringing in the depths of my memory.

A story from *The Transmission of the Lamp*, a text filled with Zen stories and sermons, illustrates the role that nature can play when a person feels its connection to the spiritual life. "A monk eager to learn Zen addressed his master and said: 'I have been newly initiated into the brotherhood. Will you be gracious enough to show me the way to Zen?' The master replied: 'Do you hear the murmuring sound of the mountain stream?' The monk answered: 'Yes, I do.'

The master said, 'Here is the entrance.'"[1]

In Zen teaching the inner life merges with the mountain stream, the flower, or the stone and becomes a spiritual path. This does not issue from any reflection or activity on our part, but flows from the awareness of a complete identification with the natural world that undercuts all intellectual distinctions. It is unnecessary to project a divine importance on things but simply allow them to be what they are; their very existence will give off a radiance.

As I relax at the side of the creek, my life ripens and my consciousness widens in the warmth of the afternoon sun. I remind myself to be present to the call of birds, the gurgle of the stream, the rising of the sun, and take full pleasure in the experience. This is enough; nothing more is necessary. A scholar and a Zen master were walking along a mountain path where a wild laurel was blooming. "The master said: 'Do you smell the fragrance of the flowering tree?' The scholar responded: 'Yes, I do.' 'Then,' declared the master, 'I have hidden nothing from you.'"[2]

Some people limit experiences of solitude and prayer to buildings away from natural surroundings and treat nature as a distraction. Occasionally they venture into the country but have little realization of what it means to allow the great rhythms of the seasons, the transformation of day to night, the presence of forest, mountain, and streams to penetrate one's existence. After seeing the Swiss Alps, Carl Jung was so awed that he called them a magic circle, a rhythmic movement of Earth, where a person could find meaning even in the middle of chaos.

The sense of unity between ourselves and the natural world is not as illusive as some would think. We normally live our lives in tune with the rhythm of nature without being conscious of it. The rhythm of work and rest parallels that of day and night; the cycle of the seasons is connected to the cycle of human life and the cycle of the liturgy. The rhythm of a woman's body finds its counterpart in the rhythm of the new moon and the full moon. To hoe the garden and watch plants emerge from the loam, struggling to make their way to the sun, is to sense one's own struggle from birth to old age, from spiritual darkness to light.

Philosopher Martin Heidegger would retreat often to a small ski hut at the side of a mountain in the southern Black Forest to think and to write. The first few hours in the cabin, he says, brought back the power of the questions he had been considering and transported him into the rhythm of his work. That the landscape nourished his existence and his work is evident in this poetic description:

> Strictly speaking I myself never observe the landscape. I experience its hourly changes, day and night, in the great comings and goings of the seasons. The gravity of the mountains and the hardness of their primeval rock, the slow

and deliberate growth of the fir-trees, the brilliant, simple splendor of the meadows in bloom, the rush of the mountain brook in the long autumn night, the stern simplicity of the flatlands covered with snow—all of this moves and flows through and penetrates daily existence up there, and not in forced moments of aesthetic immersion or artificial empathy, but only when one's own existence stands in its work.[3]

Imagine having the patience to remain in a landscape you love for a long period of time, to allow nature's supple rhythms to pervade mind and body. The heart merges with the landscape; from dawn to dusk you lose yourself in a mysterious rhythm. Slowly, a transformation occurs; anxieties are healed and thoughts begin to flow easily and spontaneously, skirting the edges of chaos. There is a greater ability to concentrate and an unexpected rush of creative power. More important, consciousness flows to a deeper level where the things in ordinary life no longer hold attraction. This, you realize, is the beginning of a contemplative state where the pressures of the practical world become a faint memory and the intuitive qualities of the soul begin to awaken.

I have found that a contemplative state uncovered in nature does not collapse under the pressure of daily city life but remains—even if it is forgotten—at the base of the being, reminding one of deeper resources for relationship and prayer. In the utter stillness and solitude of nature, under the open sky, you begin to feel a harmony with yourself, the world, and God that marks your soul for a long time.

"Whatever peace I know rests in the natural world, in feeling myself a part of it, even in a small way," writes May Sarton in her *Journal of a Solitude*.[4] Thomas Merton agrees: "One has to be alone, under the sky, before everything falls into place and one finds his own place in the midst of it all."[5] When the air vibrates with autumn stillness, who has not bathed in it, allowing the mind to settle without effort into a hidden center where the tide of silence inundates the heart? In answer to those who questioned him about the loneliness of his retreat in the mountains, Heidegger explained: "Solitude has the peculiar and original power not of isolating us but of projecting our whole existence out into the vast nearness of the presence of all things."[6] How easy it is to take for granted the power that nature has to expand consciousness beyond the boundaries of self-interest so that relationships can develop—particularly relationships with nature and those people we choose to remember. Far from hindering the activity of the human spirit nature intensifies it, acting as a sounding board for the soul's longing both for wholeness and happiness.

At one time I was unaware of the depth that was possible in a relationship between nature and prayer. I appreciated natural surroundings but thought of their influence as secondary. Nature was a beautiful, serene background, a stage for prayer and reflection, but nothing more. On one occasion in particular I discovered how limited my vision had become. I had found an ideal spot along the creek to relax and meditate late on a summer afternoon. I watched the water curl along the sandy bank; the silence was broken only by an occasional breeze and the soft sound of the ripples opening and closing around rocks. Deeply relaxed, I began to focus my attention inward. Suddenly, on a branch just above my head a blackbird let out a full-throated warble and the energy of the song filled my being completely. I looked at the shimmering water and the vast blue sky as if for the first time and felt the immediacy of God's presence both without and within. I was convinced that my prayer rose with the song of a blackbird and glided on the back of glistening water.

St. Marcus of Egypt, born around 300 A.D., insists, "If you seek God in the depth, you find him there—if you seek God in the water, there you find him—if you seek him in the fire, you will find him there also. God is everywhere, both under Earth and above the heavens and within us, too."[7] I am a beginner who takes these words to heart, attempting to find God along the edges of a creek and in the sweet smell of a forest breeze.

You cannot remain an observer of the natural world very long when you turn outward in prayer. Your participation gathers impetus from faith in

God's love and propels you into the thick of a relationship where involvement is no longer an option but a necessity. At the center of this relationship you awaken to a correspondence between the spiritual life and the natural world.

The greatest Italian landscape painter of the later fifteenth century, Giovanni Bellini, developed his own vision of correspondences between human and natural worlds. In a famous depiction of St. Francis of Assisi at prayer, *St. Francis in Ecstasy,* he brings the viewer so completely into the scene with details of rock forms, vegetation, and sky that he makes one feel that there is a harmonious and intimate relationship between Francis's spirituality and the environment. The landscape does not fade into the background as if it were unimportant, but reflects vibrantly the earthiness of Francis's spiritual experience. A drama unfolds between the landscape and the spiritual dignity of the saint. "For this visible world, with all its host and being," declares Jacob Boehme, "is nothing other than a counter-stroke of the spiritual world...."[8]

There is certainly a difference between the depth of nature's reality and the depth of the human spirit. Nevertheless, both are mysteriously related, and when nature truly engages the heart each crosses over into the other. Anyone who spends enough time in the woods, for example, finds that constants like trees, plants, rocks, sun, darkness, and light penetrate the unconscious and become charged with meaning.

Since they are experienced without the usual reflexive awareness, these images seep into the soul and become a reservoir of unexpected energy. They have the power to draw the consciousness out of isolation and into prayer. Thomas of Celano, an early biographer of St. Francis, writes that the saint "was often filled with a wonderful and ineffable joy...when he looked upon the sun, while he beheld the moon, and while he gazed at the stars...."[9]

However, those who are preoccupied with preserving their own identities will be too interested in separateness to allow a relationship with nature to grow into something pervaded by the Spirit of God. Relationship is the key. It involves giving oneself fully to the divine center of physical reality, even if the other is a horse or perhaps a stone. This kind of giving uncovers a mutual love, and a world porous with love. New images for the spiritual journey rise from the unconscious; words like Earth, sky, and wind become potent, laden with meaning and mystery; and we awaken to the power and depth of our own spirit.

It may sound simple—turn outward and remain open to the power and mystery of the natural world—but is it? Where does a relationship with nature lead? "When you are by yourself," observes Merton, "you soon get tired of your craziness. It is too exhausting. It does not fit in with the eminent sanity of trees, birds, water, sky."[10] Nature's reality uncovers a heightened sense of self, a self that we usually try to evade. Who wants to enter the woods or walk along

the shore and hear the echo of one's faltering relationship with God? "We walk to lakes to see our serenity
reflected in them," says Thoreau. "When we are not
serene, we go not to them."[11] What is God asking of
you? Remain in a landscape and listen, say Merton
and Thoreau.

Alone in the woods, I see the veil of illusion part
just enough to be aware of a self that is false. I become sensitive to the direction of my life and the suffering of others. A spirit of truth pervades my heart
and influences my words and plans. Only one thing
becomes important—the nearness of God. Each time I
return to the woods, this spiritual vulnerability sur-
prises me and effectively focuses my attention on the
important values in my life.

Turning outward to discover a path of prayer may
be difficult for some today because it is less familiar
than the traditional journey inward. We are familiar
with the struggle to find God in the depths of the
soul, but hesitate at a prayer that embraces the world
and confidently appreciates God at the heart of physical reality.

From around the fifteenth century, appreciation of
the goodness and beauty of physical reality was ignored for a more inward and individualistic devotional path. One of the classic models for the inward
way at the time could be found in *The Imitation of
Christ* written by the monk Thomas à Kempis. *The Imitation* advocated disciplining the body, the site of im-

moderate appetites, and withdrawing from the distraction of creation in order to focus on a relationship with God. The physical realities of both the self and nature were left underdeveloped in order to concentrate on the inner life. An incarnational form of prayer that affirmed the value and integrity of nature and the human body and found a path to God through the beauty and wonder of the world was excluded from the spiritual life.

In her study of *The Imitation of Christ*, along with other devotional texts, Margaret Miles explores how these manuals affected the people who read them. She forgoes judging the ideas, attitudes, and values represented in the texts, and instead interprets them with a discerning eye, uncovering their limited value for spirituality today. She comes to the conclusion that transcendence of the body and nature and concentration on the soul as the true focus of spiritual attention may have been attractive to people at certain times and places, but "This interpretation of human transcendence has substantially contributed to creating the nuclear world, a world more literally 'despised' than even the harshest medieval ascetic could have imagined."[12] In her conclusion she suggests:

> Instead of interpreting human transcendence in the direction of its potential for body-denying, world-rejecting escapism, we must reinterpret transcendence, not only as individual self-awareness but also as recognition of the interde-

pendence of all living beings. Christians must locate ideas and images—surely not an impossible task in the religion of the Incarnation, the Word made flesh—that help us, perhaps for the first time in the history of Christianity, fully to value, cherish, and treasure the natural world.[13]

The foolishness of our inherited mistrust of the natural world as a path to God is dramatically evident when we are confronted by the concrete reality of nature; the majesty and power of the Atlantic or Pacific Ocean or the delicate scent of a pine grove on a warm summer afternoon. Who can concentrate on the inward journey to the exclusion of all else while walking along the shore or following a path into the Rocky Mountains? These encounters with nature, if we are awake enough to take them seriously, quickly draw us outside ourselves and pull us toward a path of prayer that complements the inward movement of the spirit.

There is a story told of Cuthbert, the first Roman bishop of Lindisfarne and head of a monastery, who thoroughly immersed himself in the Celtic disposition toward prayer, solitude, and nature. After preaching to a group of nuns one day, Cuthbert went to the beach to pray. He walked into the cold water until the waves reached his chest, and then, with arms raised to the heavens, he spent the night in prayer. At dawn he left the water and collapsed on the beach while otters played at his feet. Cuthbert ended his vigil by blessing the otters and sending them back into the water. A monk who had followed him related the incident to others.[14]

Jesus himself was not afraid to stand chest deep in creation when he prayed to the Father. He entered the waters of the Jordan River to begin his divine sonship and emerged, his life transformed in the Spirit. His parables ring with the voice of one who was intimate with nature, who knew the mysterious contours of the desert landscape that he inhabited for forty days. He often found it necessary to find seclusion in the silence of nature to refresh his spirit after preaching: "And when he had sent the multitudes away, he went up into a mountain apart to pray: and when evening came he was there alone" (Matthew 14:23–24). It is easy to imagine that he was exhausted by the crowds and sought refuge in lonely places, but it is also obvious that he chose natural settings beyond the towns and villages as refuge for prayer.

The early desert fathers and mothers of Egypt and Palestine and the *poustiniks* of Russia's forests and deserts knew the intimate connection between nature and the spiritual life. They were earthy people whose writings included references to common, everyday considerations like eating, sleeping, and a place to live. They chose the wilderness not only because of the distraction of large cities but because the power and mystery of their natural environment focused their lives of prayer. In our own time, Charles de Foucald, Thomas Merton, and others have followed their footsteps into natural settings.

From a purely rational point of view, it may seem that the inward and outward ways of prayer contradict one another, but on an experiential level the contradiction is illusory. Francis of Assisi, for example, is well known for a way of prayer that embraced the beauty and mystery of nature, yet he also journeyed into the depths of the heart where he took on the cross of Christ in humility and poverty. He may have rambled though the countryside singing lyrics, but he also secluded himself in caves and abandoned churches to concentrate on sorrow for his sins.

In a revealing study of two great mystics, Meister Eckhart and Sankara, Rudolph Otto describes the differences between the inward way and the way of unity and suggests that these two tendencies merge so completely in the lives of mystics that they form an ideal blending of two spiritual movements, a blending which the mystics themselves considered perfectly natural.[15]

Through personal preference and through grace, each of us tends to emphasize either the inner or the outer ways of prayer. Yet, neither should be emphasized to the exclusion of the other for fear of sacrificing a balanced spiritual life. Like Augustine, we may yearn to withdraw from outward things and retreat to the ground of the soul, but like Augustine, too, we must be open to the overwhelming beauty of the natural world.

Thoreau advises: "Open all your pores and bathe

in all the tides of Nature, in all her streams and oceans, at all seasons."[16] It is never enough to take nature at face value. In knowing nature deeply you know the God who created her, and experience the love that flows not only within your heart but throughout the world. Incarnational prayer is not just the appreciation of the goodness and wonder of physical reality but the willingness to allow ourselves to find deep joy in it, to love it truthfully in God. If you find your own imagination lacking, try to picture what nature might have looked like through the eyes of someone who saw it differently; like Christ, St. Francis, Thomas Merton, Henry David Thoreau, Julian of Norwich, or Hildegärd of Bingen. Each of them found the holy in nature and marveled at the love reflected in created reality. Each gazed at the natural world until words fell away and only a divine presence remained.

Perhaps the most dramatic example of what it means to find a spiritual unity with the natural world in this late twentieth century comes from women who have proclaimed the mystery of the female body and who have discovered in both the body and nature a dwelling place for the divine. Women have gone into the deep pool of their imaginations, beyond the levels of traditional patriarchal images, and emerged with new images rooted in the flesh and earth—images dripping with primal power like moon, water, tree, and soil. In a lecture, "Women at Prayer," Mary Collins refers to this spiritual journey as it is represented in the work of a contemporary contemplative artist, Meinrad Craighead: "With the gift of awareness she calls her 'subterranean' source, she plants us firmly back on Earth, and invites us into the mystery of the female body. She finds both earth and body to be good and the dwelling place of the God whose face we seek."[17]

Why a prayer that involves a relationship with nature? Isn't it because nature comes to reflect the silence, beauty, and truth which we find in our own hearts? Even the simple act of entering a landscape can become an act of worship, and seeing a sunrise from a car window can inspire reverent adoration of God. But only those who have taken the turn outward seriously can appreciate the power contained in the simple prayer of gazing upon the morning sun and finding one's heart addressed by God. Nature sometimes reveals a voice so overwhelming that we are stunned and stand in awe, not believing that the world can so dramatically tell us of God's nearness.

It is no secret that God speaks the loudest when we are ready to hear. These may be times when we are burned out from work and activity and our lives feel frantic and lost. During these times we may head for the woods or the shore or the mountains for a brief retreat and find that we slip into the arms of nature like a child coming to rest in the arms of a mother. The soft breezes and warmth of the sun, the smells of Earth, and the sound of trees rocking in a breeze comfort us. Nature gently coaxes us back into God's presence. This is an experience that all of us have had at one time or another. We returned refreshed and re-focused on the deeper values of our lives, and sur-prised at the depth and spontaneity of our prayer.

As I sit at the side of this creek on the lime-green grass deep in the valley, a weight is taken from my shoulders. Little Salmon Creek is clear and innocent, lacking the sophistication of larger streams with their heavy waters and murky banks. It ushers me into a simpler world filled with dreams and promises. I read that St. Ignatius of Loyola was at the side of a stream contemplating the movement of the water when "the eyes of his mind were opened, not so as to see any kind of vision, but so as to understand and comprehend spiritual things...and this with such clearness that for him all these things were made new."[18] What more could one ask for? The flow of the creek introduces possibilities both within and beyond nature; its flowing water baptizes and renews vision. Creek song rushes into the caverns of my uncon-scious, drawing me homeward.

2

Awakening to
the Call of Beauty

One of the most important—and most neglected—elements in the beginnings of the interior life is the ability to respond to reality, to see the value and the beauty in ordinary things, to come alive to the splendor that is all around us....

Thomas Merton

There is a story about an ancient Hindu king who possessed great wealth but began to be haunted by feelings that his wealth meant nothing. He became eager to meditate on eternal truths and went to a yogi for advice. During his meditation he found that he could not keep his mind on eternal matters; his attention repeatedly returned to a magnificent bracelet he wore, which he deeply admired. The more he tried to refocus his attention, the harder it became to take his mind off the bracelet; so, in humility he returned to the yogi for advice. Realizing that prayer can take many forms, the yogi told him, "Since your mind is so much attached to the bracelet, start right there. Meditate upon the bracelet. Contemplate its beauty and brilliant colors. Then inquire into the source of that beauty and those colors."[1]

Meditation on the bracelet in this story gives us an idea of what it means to meditate on the beauty of nature. A flash of natural beauty catches the eye—autumn leaves shimmering with frost on the forest floor or a quiet sycamore revealing whiteness in the ripening sunlight—and we become haunted by the thought of beauty itself and passionately crave it, searching the world with the eyes of a pilgrim. Revelations of beauty feed our soul like swollen currents feed a river. Yet, all the time, we realize that ultimate beauty can exist only in God, and our longing becomes our prayer.

Many, however, remain afraid of this path through the world, feeling that the multiplicity and the attraction of beautiful things should be ignored in favor of a more secure, spiritual path. Petrarch, one of the first people in modern time to move from the chaos of the city to enjoy the peace and beauty of the countryside, climbed a mountain, as the story goes, simply to enjoy the view. While admiring the Mediterranean and the Rhône at his feet, he felt inclined to open St. Augustine's *Confessions* and found this passage: "And men go about to wonder at the heights of mountains...but themselves they consider not." He closed the book, angry with himself for concentrating on earthly things when he should have been tending to his soul, and descended the mountain in tight-lipped silence.[2]

Does spiritual growth occur by suppressing our passion for nature's beauty, or by allowing the passion to be transformed by God? Augustine himself, though interested primarily in a world-transcending, platonic ascent of the soul in his early years, embraced the biblical, world-affirming perspective toward creation in his later years, and wrote that the created order was transparent to the beauty and wisdom of God for those whose affections were properly ordered.[3] Mystics, such as Meister Eckhart, warn us that pursuing God in nature rather than our own desires is not something that comes naturally. It does demand a degree of detachment and humility. Yet, a Christian is not called to ignore nature and her creatures, but only to bring under control the possessiveness that causes us to exploit the natural world for our own ends.

One thing is certain: Discovering God in the beauty and grace of the world is not a path that we hear enough about. For this reason, it is all the more necessary to learn to enjoy the beauty of nature and allow the experience to become prayer and nourish our spiritual lives. Perhaps the difficulty is not that we love the beauty of the world, but that we do not love it deeply enough.

The path of beauty was familiar to each of us from early childhood, when we allowed ourselves to be enchanted by the pattern and color of autumn leaves as we gathered them for a school assignment, or when we stayed out late at night catching fireflies and came under the spell of a full moon. In childhood the beauty of a summer's day became an invitation to explore the unknown.

When I was a child my parents moved to the country for a few years. I walked the long fields, picked berries, followed the creeks till dusk, and lost myself exploring in the forest. I remember the farm as a home and an adventure. I felt that my life was wide enough to include Earth and sky; that I belonged in the fields and in the boughs of apple trees. When I look back now I realize that at the time images of the natural world were taking root in my soul; I belonged to the land.

Years later, after the childhood sensitivity to nature gave way to more practical considerations, I found myself returning to the forest, walking the paths endlessly, drawn by the calmness of trees and the wildness of the landscape. I wanted to know things in the deepest way possible, to appreciate the beauty of trees, the creeks, the sky, and Earth. The yearning to find something more in the beauty of nature became an unquenchable thirst, and the beauty of the forest began to echo my hunger for God. The image of the forest that had remained dormant from my early youth once again surfaced with power. It was no longer a child's fancy but a cipher of the soul; nature's beauty was echoing an inner call.

The importance of this heightened sensitivity toward the natural world, now that I am able to reflect on it, was that it marked the beginning of a journey to know God. How humbling it is to recognize that God spoke through the wild things of creation at a time when I was most open to their story. Each thing was a word of God, and together they formed a hypnotic language that echoed a strange, new dialogue between me and God.

Each time I enter the forest now I am reminded of an inner call. The wind roaring through the treetops, the rain pattering on leaves, the stillness at the center of a wild landscape—all of these communicate the soul's longing. My forest journey has become a spiritual adventure that finds its origins in childhood memories and continues to this day.

How does a passion for beauty and grace awaken in us? It begins with faith in the presence of God at the heart of the natural world, a presence that may at any time reveal itself through the beauty of forms. Through faith we remain open to participation in nature. This is a serious commitment, one that should not be taken lightly. As St. Bonaventure warns:

Whoever, therefore, is not enlightened
by such splendor of created things is blind;
whoever is not awakened by such outcries
    is deaf....
Therefore, open your eyes,
alert the ears of your spirit, open your lips
and apply your heart....lest the whole world
    rise against you.[4]

We may wake up, if only briefly, from the sleep of daily life to hear the call of beauty. We then become more and more vulnerable to the beauty of nature and begin to love things we did not expect to love: the stillness of trees, green stalks, dolphins, wild woods, and a broom of yellow flowers.

Participation in the natural world brings feelings of peace and calm; it is like the tranquil spirit of a gardener who tills the soil and works close to nature for long periods of time. "...everything that slows us down and forces patience, everything that sets us back into the slow cycles of nature, is a help. Gardening is an instrument of grace," writes May Sarton in her journal.[5] The more familiar we are with beauty and grace—small miracles of light on the water, a child at play in long green fields, a fire on a dark beach while moonlight dances in the surf—the more we will appreciate the rhythms of the natural world as something truly good for the human spirit.

Thomas Merton was startled one day by his own vision of beauty. It came during his pilgrimage to

Asia, where he found an unexpected stimulus for his contemplative vision. On the island of Sri Lanka, at Polonnaruwa, Merton visited giant stone statues of Buddha near a rock outcropping. He approached the figures barefoot and with reserve, soaking in the silence that poured out of the rock and caves. He was astonished at the peaceful smiles and noticed that the shape and line of the statues seemed to merge with the rocks and trees of the landscape. Contemplating the scene, he was shocked out of his usual habit of perception: The rock came alive and the figures of Buddha took on an overwhelming clarity and power.

Merton found peace and an intuition of beauty within the experience: "All problems are resolved and everything is clear, simply because what matters is clear. The rock, all matter, all life, were charged with *dharmakaya*....everything is emptiness and everything is compassion. I don't know when in my life I have ever had such a sense of beauty and spiritual validity running together in one aesthetic illumination."[6]

For some, the call of beauty may begin a spiritual pilgrimage that continues for a lifetime. This was the case for Rollo May, the renowned psychiatrist.[7] May was a young teacher living in Greece when he began to suffer extreme fatigue. In an attempt to recover from the exhaustion, he took some time away from teaching and journeyed up a large mountain where he found a room above a small cafe. During his stay he undertook a process of self-analysis, trying to discover a focus for his life. On the way down the mountain he became so enraptured with a hillside of wild poppies that he sat among them and drew their forms. Suddenly, he realized how deaf he had been to an inner voice that spoke to him of spiritual beauty, and how his life had become so practical and work-oriented that he never found the time to enjoy nature. This insight began a personal devotion to art and beauty that, only a month later, led to the monasteries of Mt. Athos. While journeying from monastery to monastery he found himself ignoring the monks and his companions and concentrating almost entirely on the lavish beauty of the mountains. Contemplating the orange blossoms, pine groves, and mountain streams, he saw that nature worshiped God and offered a glimpse of eternity. His spiritual hunger temporarily sated, he knew that he would travel the path of beauty for the rest of his life.

It seems that May's experience accurately parallels our own at different times in our lives. We become so immersed in the serious business of life, our minds preoccupied and our bodies exhausted, that we can drive to work in the morning and forget to notice the beauty of the world around us. Yet, in our hearts we seek a place to rest, a place where we can sink into nature and into the depths of our own souls.

In childhood, Bede Griffiths also heard an extraordinary and captivating call of beauty that would eventually lead him on a lifelong journey of faith:

It came to me quite suddenly, as it were out of the blue, and now that I look back on it, it seems to me that it was one of the decisive events of my life. Up to that time I had lived the life of a normal schoolboy, quite content with the world as I found it. Now I was suddenly made aware of another world of beauty and mystery such as I had never imagined to exist, except in poetry. It was as though I had begun to see and smell and hear for the first time.[8]

Throughout his youth, Griffiths's love for nature ran deep, and he sought solitude in the woods and hills. He continued to uncover a reality that lay behind the face of nature, and read both philosophy and theology to determine more about this power within the universe. He found not only beauty and truth beneath the surface of nature, but also a moral power that made demands on him and that he perceived as personal. During a time of conflict and conversion, he recalls, "God brought me to my knees and made me acknowledge my own nothingness, and out of that knowledge I was reborn. I was no longer the center of my life and therefore I could see God in everything."[9]

Later, Griffiths entered a monastic order and found that his mature belief allowed him to see nature differently, with new eyes; everything had a sacramental character. He experienced a harmony with nature and with the rhythm of the seasons. All distance between him and the natural world vanished, and he felt that he participated in a universal order for all things.

Spiritual journeys that include an awareness of God as infinite Beauty can be traced in Christian tradition at least as far back as the Celtic Christian monasticism in fifth-century Ireland. The Celtic monasteries embraced a spirituality that included a sensitivity to the beauty of the fields, forests, rivers, and seas. Even though the physical environment could be harsh and unforgiving, the lush green countryside of Ireland revealed God's love, care, and gentleness.

Not long after Patrick arrived in Ireland, Celtic spirituality reached an apex. New monasteries were built in places of wild, natural beauty, and saints like Columba came to the forefront. It was a time when individuals were inspired to leave behind everything in the name of Christ and embark on pilgrimages. Many of these wandering hermits and monks changed the face of Ireland because they shared a unique spirituality in their relationships with kings and creatures. These evangelical monks wrote poems, and established monasteries in places of wild, natural beauty. Their prayerful pilgrimages, which embraced nature, provided models for many after them who would embark on similar spiritual journeys.[10]

Holy men and women throughout history have mapped the way for our own pilgrimage toward God through the beauty of the natural world. Julian of Norwich, for example, affirmed the beauty and goodness of each created thing because it represented the abundant graciousness of God. Francis of Assisi found that his identification with the passion of Christ allowed him to see divine life in all created reality. Ignatius of Loyola encouraged us to meditate on the active, dynamic presence of God in nature. Hildegärd of Bingen opened her arms to creation as an expression of grace. Teilhard de Chardin invited us to experience an incarnational God at the heart of the universe. Abraham Heschel reminded us that the world is radiant with beauty and grace, and that our truest response is one of awe and wonder. Perhaps Meister Eckhart summarizes all of these paths best when he concludes: "This then is salvation: to marvel at the beauty of created things and praise the beautiful providence of their Creator."[11]

Gerard Manley Hopkins saw beauty in the wild aspects of nature rather than in her tame or domestic forms: "What would the world be, once bereft of wet and of wilderness?... Long live the weeds and the wilderness yet."[12] Those who read Hopkins's poetry will find little indication of an orderly nature but rather a nature bursting at the seams with a profusion of riches and an unending variety of forms. He prefers taking us through a multitude of "dappled" and "mottled" things on our journey to oneness with God. Perhaps he believed that wild beauty more readily reflected the heart's longing for God.

I remember reading that Albert Schweitzer left cultivated soil and set foot in the formless wild of a jungle landscape of Africa. The power of the wilderness must have reinforced the longing of his soul for spiritual truths or he would have retreated to tamer land. John Muir, the naturalist, is well known for his preference for the spiritual refreshment of wild places. Having arrived in San Francisco by way of a Panama steamer, he asked a stranger for the nearest way out of town. "Well, where do you want to go?" asked the stranger. "To any place that is wild," replied Muir.[13]

I, too, prefer the forest chaos of green, the gnarled roots, and the rugged contour of Earth. When I enter the deep woods my heart grows heavy with longing, and the beauty of the wild seduces me into being watchful and fruitful. Forest wilderness awakens a desire for the dark and shoreless self, the self that lies beyond social life, beyond routine, and beyond rational thought. The paths, rough and unpredictable, lure me deeper and deeper into the woods. I imagine walking until I am lost, forgetting plans and attending to spiritual frontiers that I have forgotten.

In an essay describing his journey into the Red River Gorge of the Daniel Boone National Forest of Kentucky, Wendell Berry sketches a broad outline of wilderness that rings true because it reflects the wilderness that each of us carries inside ourselves:

Wilderness is the element in which we live encased in civilization, as a mollusk lives in his shell in the sea. It is a wilderness that is beautiful, dangerous, abundant, oblivious of us, mysterious, never to be conquered or controlled or second-guessed, or known more than a little. It is a wilderness that for most of us most of the time is kept out of sight, camouflaged, by the edifices and the busyness and the bothers of human society.[14]

When the passion for beauty takes us beneath appearances, we suddenly discover that beauty shares in divine life. It becomes a symbol. As a symbol, nature is most real because it reflects the sacred dimension of the world.

The warmth of the sun means little to me when I live close to a warm shelter; but when I camp in the woods during autumn I wake chilled to the bone and immediately look for a spot in a clearing where the light will splash down as the sun rises over the mountain tops. Sitting against a tree, basking in the first warmth of the day, my skin grows flush and I watch the warm glance of the sun unleash a fine mist in the high grass. At times like these, when I feel the immediacy and power of the sun's influence, I realize that it possesses more reality than I had thought. The sun is a gift not to be taken for granted; it contains the power of life and is the source of grace. Without it I could not survive.

To experience the warmth of the sun after the chill of night is to discover a symbol. No artificial separation between the reality of nature and nature as a

symbol can exist when the beauty and power of sunlight introduces you to a multi-dimensional world.

Medieval theologians have called this symbolic
world a "language" or an expression of the mind of
God. They saw the script of beauty writ large in the
sun, moon, and stars:

The heavens proclaim your glory, O God, and the
firmament shows forth the work of your hands. Day
carries the news to day, and night brings the message
to night (Psalm 19:2–3).

As language, the world is more similar to poetry
than to a scientific treatise. It has depth, resonance,
and profound meaning. The Hebrews said *dabhar*
(word) and they did not mean a one-dimensional reality; they were referring to the creative energy of
God that penetrates all beings and gives birth to creation.

In one of his sermons Meister Eckhart proclaims,
"All created things are God's speech and manifest the
same as does my mouth about God."[15] Power to communicate is hidden in all of nature. The wind wash-
ing through the boughs, the rain splashing on leaves,
a bird singing at dawn in the stillness of dark trees—
all of these have potential to communicate in ways
we do not expect. We are influenced by the images of
nature, whether we are conscious of it or not.

The broad sky, lush foliage, and fertile earth are
archetypes rooted in the history of the human consciousness; they are entrances into the forces that
work in the human soul. "These great images (earth,

sun, moon, water, air, fire)," writes Eloi Leclerc, "have the power to draw consciousness out of its isolation and put it in contact with the transcendent fullness of life."[16] Feeling the world's holiness in the marrow of his bones, Francis of Assisi lets out a shout of praise: "Praise be to you, my Lord, with all your creatures,/Especially Sir Brother Sun..." ("The Canticle of Brother Sun").

We call nature beautiful, but we also know that she is riddled with death and decay, and her power can be destructive. Rain falling in waves, tops of trees shaking, and branches crashing to the ground in a gale, or hailstones as big as marbles remind us of nature's unpredictability. I remember camping one night and waking to flashes of lightning and rolling peals of thunder. The sides of the tent sucked in and blew out and sheets of rain whipped against the top. Looking out a small nylon mesh window, I could see the flickering of light in the dark, open sky. Nature wreaked havoc with my sense of security. The next morning I sat and listened to the rain dripping from the trees and I felt very fragile.

Those whose livelihood depends on nature know her power to destroy firsthand, as do those whose lives have been threatened by floods, hurricanes, tornadoes, or earthquakes. Each autumn we are reminded that nature is a broken place and not paradise. There is a best to nature but there is also a worst.

Neither of these two sides should be dismissed.

They make up nature's reality and represent our experience. Also, both sides are closely intertwined: Nature's beauty, for example, is intimate with her death. Hopkins expresses this insight in his poem, "Hurrahing in Harvest," where the death of summer is described as a time when nature is "barbarous in beauty."[17] Each of us has, on occasion, realized that the extravagant colors of autumn are an expression of death. We are dumbstruck by overwhelming beauty but realize that nature is ephemeral. What should our response be? What do we say to the beauty of a world threatened by death and decay?

In his book *Night Country*, Loren Eisley describes a walk along the beach where he witnesses a broken-winged gull close to death and a wild duck, also with a broken wing, trying to escape into the water. As he watches, the duck slowly and painfully moves into the water and is finally overcome by the waves. He reflects that this is the way it was before humanity: "This is the chaos before man came, before sages imbued with pity walked Earth. God's ways are mystery to us; God's order seems chaos to us."[18]

Like Job we behold death and destruction and we find ourselves wailing in the darkness. We walk the beach corridor or a forest path and discover that our lack of understanding and sense of fragility turn us to a God whose ways are truly mysterious. We make the shift from independence to dependence on God and find that nature no longer frightens and confuses but reveals a unique, hidden beauty. Through her vulnerablity, Earth calls us beyond this world to the rich fullness of divine life: "...resting first on the things that you have made, and passing on to you who made those things in so wonderful a way," writes Augustine.[19]

During a recent camping trip I became acutely aware of the signs of decay and death around me; trees rotting, leaves turning brown, insects eating other insects, the constant irrational changes in the environment. Dead tree trunks stretched over the creek became the only thing I saw. The second day, I found my eyes resting on the stillness of a pond; my soul expanded and filled with silence. The silence broke easily on my consciousness, and I sat in the stillness thinking of my vulnerability and how dependent I was on God's love.

Nature plies the heart just as the desolate Sinai Desert molded the stiff hearts of the Hebrews and caused a prayer to issue from their mouths. As the Israelites trudged through the desert they discovered a reality that every Bedouin knows: There is no room in the desert for pretense. The heat of day and the cold of night will remind you at every turn that your attention should be directed toward someone greater than yourself.

> I look at your heavens, the work of your hands,
> at the moon and stars which you created—
> who are we that you should be mindful of us,
> that you should care for us? (Psalm 8:4,5)

In the end, an awareness of beauty and grace is always a surprise. You suddenly notice in a glance of light that grace appears in its own way and in its own time. You ask yourself how it is possible that this particular form of a tree shifting in the evening light or the sound of birdsong in a breeze can evoke such feelings of reverence and awe. You conclude that nature's beauty is mystery and there is nothing to do but remain open to the surprise. It was said of Francis of Assisi that, "In beautiful things he saw Beauty itself; all things were to him good."[20]

We are truly gifted creatures, but sometimes we wait too long to recognize this. "Too late have I loved you, O Beauty, so ancient and so new, too late have I loved you!" laments St. Augustine.[21] We can't stand the heat of God's nearness in the world, so we tend to hide our days in business. In the meantime we hear the intimations of beauty in a pacific breeze, in the flutter of wings, and in every rocky crevice where a flower grows. There are times when we know that God is speaking personally to us through the beauty of a flower or the warm glance of sun on the napes of our necks; these are times when the natural world captures the spiritual imagination and leads us on an adventure into the unknown.

It is no secret that the ancient passion for beauty and grace in the world expresses the soul's deep longing for happiness. Exploring this passion leads many to Beauty itself, where it is discovered that all is grace; nature is grace, and the soul's capacity to know God through nature is grace. Even later, when the revelation of beauty fades, when the doe in the meadow with steam rising from her flanks disappears into the woods, the eye still glows from this brush with innocence and memory stores it for future contemplation.

3

Waiting for Dawn

I arise today
Through the strength of heaven:
Light of sun,
Radiance of moon,
Splendor of fire,
Speed of lightning,
Swiftness of wind,
Depth of sea,
Stability of earth,
Firmness of rock.

St. Patrick, "The Deer's Cry"

In the preceding chapters we have been describing the first stages of a prayer that turns outward and finds a path to God through the mystery and beauty of the natural world. In the next two chapters, a prelude to encountering the silence and light of nature, I would like to introduce two responses to the natural world that are essential nourishment for this prayer: wonder and reverence. Let us turn our attention first to wonder.

When I think of a time of wonder, a time when I am most aware of a mysterious relationship with the natural world, I think of the moments just before dawn, when daylight consciousness has not yet emerged. I recall lying awake in the tent, waiting for the first signs of light to appear in the forest. Above the tent, leaves skitter about in the wash of a morning breeze; off to the side, I hear Little Salmon Creek crashing over small rocks. Sound intensifies in the stillness, and I imagine the lush green of the forest surrounding me and the transparent water of the creek winding through the darkness.

I dress and leave the tent while it is still dark. A thick mist covers the valley; the rain cloth wrapped over the tent is buckling under the weight of moisture. Vague patches of gray are beginning to appear along the boundaries of the clearing. In time, tree skeletons will emerge, foliage will turn bold green, and the sand at the side of the creek will frost with light. I have watched this transformation many times, and each time I am aware of the expansiveness of my being. How easily consciousness mingles with the emerging forms of early morning, allowing me to see them fresh and vibrant!

It is a shame that we tend to ignore morning's half-light when consciousness is just surfacing. From second to second, we slowly wake up, pull away from the deeper ties we have with nature and people, and allow daylight consciousness to take control. We slip from our moorings in the unconscious, drift from its wild swirling waters into a more tame and controlled existence. In a short time, midday consciousness effectively filters out the memory of the powerful and fertile bond with people and nature that we carry hidden within. Only when we have lost contact with a person or a place do we realize how much we have forgotten.

We are truly in communion with nature, but this is not something that we know fully. At first it is an intuition, a vague sense that somehow all the tangible universe—stars, earth, and seas—are reproduced within us. This is not a feeling that people readily put into words, so we need the intuition reinforced in us by the experiences and words of saints, poets, artists, and astronauts.

In a book dedicated to the experiences of astronauts and cosmonauts in space, a group of Russian cosmonauts told a story about starting a garden in a space station. The small garden, especially the greenness of the plants, was so refreshing and so deeply transforming that it became a source of spiritual tranquility. Expressing the delight of the entire group, one cosmonaut, Georgi Grechko, said, "It's impossible to imagine how much pleasure this green oasis of terrestrial life gave us. We even said,

'Come on, let's walk in the grove.'"[1]

"Our relationships with our environments are not something we have but something through which we come to be," writes John Shea.[2] In the dim light of the early morning forest I think of waking for the first time to the ancient memory of leaves, stems, robins, and willows, and I take my own "walk in the grove" along the creek. I am awed and a little frightened at the way these things take form in the rising light of dawn and fill the slopes of my mind.

It occurs to me that the human spirit is unlimited. It blows through the skin and whirls us away to surprising places, engaging us in our surroundings in ways that we do not imagine. In the full light of day the self may be cupped like a shell in an attempt to preserve its identity, but in the half-light of early morning you can hear the resonances of the tides and waves of relationship. Relationships enter us and we are transformed; who cares to say where the relationship stops and the self begins?

In the innocence of childhood the world is not yet separate, and so the self extends indefinitely, reaching out to all that brings pleasure and amazement. Nature is holy, a world of wonder, rhythm, and energy. "And the sabbath rang slowly/In the pebbles of the holy streams," writes Dylan Thomas, recalling his youth.[3] In childhood the world easily mingles with the inner life; we dream and sleep under the stars filled with memories of Earth. With this vision of the world fresh in mind, a child becomes a prophet who shouts out that the emperor is naked, while the adults parade through town intent on preserving their foolish illusion.

Adults often fail to reclaim their relationship with nature and instead hold on to other prospects for happiness. In their stubbornness they sacrifice a prayer that sounds pure hosanna on behalf of the self and Earth. Yet, there are times when the usual mental categories fall away and adults unexpectedly recover their ability to dream. Antoine de Saint Exupéry remembers a time when his plane was forced down in the Sahara Desert. He fell asleep in the overwhelming silence only to awaken to a dark, immense sky with its whirling unlimited depths opening up and engulfing him. He felt himself adrift with nothing to secure his being in place, his back barely in contact with earth as he spun through the universe. He yearned for gravity as one would yearn for a friend whose support had been forgotten, then suddenly remembered and appreciated. He realized it was gravity alone that anchored his existence and kept him from floating away into the dark nothingness of the universe. Gravity—he acknowledged, humbly and joyfully—was sheer gift. Why had he not seen this before?[4]

Little Bo-Peep lost her sheep and what did she do? She sat down and waited for them to come home. We learn patience from children. When I stop struggling to make things happen and take time to rest in the thick of a forest along a stream, I learn to appreciate and enjoy life, both its harshness and beauty. I am more willing to let events unfold in their own time, without interfering. Most of all, I find myself saying—to my surprise—that this world is "very good." Faith in God's creation is faith in all life as graced. On my best days I claim with Thoreau that, "My profession is to be always on the alert to find God in nature, to know his lurking places, to attend all the oratorios, the operas...in nature."[5]

I am sitting against an ancient oak at the side of the creek. I can feel the powerful form of the tree against my back and imagine that it is a column of pure energy. The flow of energy suddenly shoots from the ground and forms each leaf in a flash of light. I look overhead and see the leaves shining in the late afternoon sun, revealing shape, texture, and hue—the entire tree pulses with light and energy, the sheer goodness of being. Jacob Boehme imagined that the sap that ran upward from the roots of a tree was pure divinity and the tree itself represented the wholeness of the universe.

Shifting through levels of time in the forest, I come to rest on some vague hint of eternity where I grasp the obscure notion of the goodness of being. I know that I dwell in time, caught in the sequence of events, but I also know that my being is not wholly contained in time. Both the temporal and the eternal intersect in me. Eternity hurls from the sky like lightning in the darkness of a storm. Suddenly the forest lights up in a pale blue light, freezing everything in one flash. I imagine that, in this moment of skittering light, temporal reality halts, the eternal transforms the temporal, and Earth becomes a place of overwhelming goodness.

One of the things that impresses me about the poet Gerard Manley Hopkins is his willingness to let go of his life in the face of mystery. Hopkins found Earth pulsing with divine love and things themselves giving off sparks and threatening to "flame out like shook foil."[6] What sudden flash of splendor did he see before his eyes? Who is this God he believed in, "charging" the world and remaining a force actively engaged in it?

Physics tells us that at the level of subatomic particles there is no sign of cause and effect; there is no predictable movement. In fact, the particles themselves seem to possess an inner rhythm; they already know their steps in the dance and they work together, not by knocking into one another and causing a chain reaction, but by listening to a secret rhythm. Nature is alive and dancing, and even the smallest bit of matter knows this; yet we persist in closing our imaginations.

Like many artists before him, photographer Ansel Adams insists, "The whole world is very much 'alive'—all the little growing things, even the rocks. I can't look at a swell bit of grass and earth, for instance, without feeling the essential life—the things going on—within them."[7]

"The deep eye sees the shimmer on the stone,"[8] writes Theodore Roethke. While walking along a road one gloomy day, Martin Buber picked up a piece of mica that had somehow caught his attention. He stared at the stone until its light overpowered the surrounding darkness. Looking away from the translucent object, he realized that he had experienced an event that cut beneath his normal sense of isolation from the world. The revelation awakened him to the richness and depth of nature and to the intensity of his own spiritual life.

The renowned theoretical physicist Freeman Dyson tells us that the field of physics has become so diverse and complicated that, to use his metaphor, "it is like wandering through the Amazon valley and quietly uncovering a plethora of life forms."[9] At one time, in the early 1920s, it was thought that the theories of relativity and the quantum had shed light and revealed a solid, discernible landscape. Now, according to Dyson, we are in the heart of the jungle, at the center of the rain forest, counting sixty-one species of elementary particles when before only three were known; six or more states of matter instead of the usual ones of solid, liquid, and gas; we are contending with innumerable mathematical structures to summarize the world of physics when previously a few equations would do.

It is as if we had been reading the first chapter of a book and felt satisfied that this was the entire story. Now we find that there are many more chapters, and we can perceive the world in a multitude of ways. The disruption of a simple material universe with its objective world of space and time, independent of human thought and observation, may seem like the concern of a laboratory scientist alone, but it affects everyone.

Living in a multi-dimensional world changes the way we see our relationship with nature and the way we see ourselves. Many, of course, choose to return to the first chapter where they can find a story they are familiar with, though they know they are settling for a severely limited vision. The discoveries of modern science are pushing us to decide whether we want to remain with a one-dimensional reality or become involved in a world of mystery and wonder.

This is a difficult choice, for it asks us to set aside our arrogance and realize that humanity is a small and humble part of a vast, mysterious universe. It is not enough to be satisfied with the fact that we have the ability to know; we must also realize the deeper truth: We are known, ultimately by God but also by nature itself.

This is exactly the point that Laurens Van der Post makes while describing the Bushmen of Africa.[10] The Bushmen, he says, believed that their lives were known by the stars and the desert. When someone died, a star would fall from the sky and tell all who would listen that a person who walked upright had fallen. We may have lost this innocent relationship with the universe forever, but the longing to be known by the stars and by God still remains in our hearts.

What do you do when terra firma begins to flow though your hands like water and it cries, "Catch me if you can"? "The world is not controllable. It is too much for us. It is crammed with marvel," exclaims Abraham Heschel.[11] If there is one thing we know for certain, according to the new physics, it is that at bottom all things are somehow inextricably related. At the center of the world we find nothing that we can control and compartmentalize, only the tensions of relationship. Thomas Merton celebrates this vision in a piece he wrote, appropriately entitled "The Dance of Life":

> For the world and time are the dance of the Lord in emptiness. The silence of the spheres is the music of a wedding feast. The more we persist in misunderstanding the phenomena of life, the more we analyze them out into strange finalities and complex purposes of our own, the more we involve ourselves in sadness, absurdity and despair. But it does not matter much, because no despair of ours can alter the reality of

things, or stain the joy of the cosmic dance
which is always there. Indeed, we are in the
midst of it, and it is in the midst of us, for it
beats in our very blood, whether we want it to
or not.[12]

The reality of this dance acted out in a fertile void,
on a stage of emptiness, should shock us into wonder. Matter is no longer to be taken for granted; it is
not fundamentally deaf and dumb. It is mystery, and
we have reason to believe that it is in some way sen-
tient. We live on a planet that is conscious, alive, and
informed with knowledge.

The Gaia hypothesis of J.E. Lovelock proposes that
earth is much more than a piece of rock, an island
reeling in a vast enigmatic space, but constitutes a living entity which has the power to regulate the salini-
ty of the seas and the level of oxygen in the atmosphere.[13] Gaia, the Greek personification of Earth as
goddess, draws our attention away from the scientist
examining the parts-per-million of a rare gas, and
turns it toward Earth of myth, who brings forth life
and is the origin of all nurturing: physical, intellectual, and spiritual.

This perception of Earth may seem strange to the
modern mind but it is not new. Mircea Eliade writes
that primordial cultures felt that the very existence of
Earth had an impact on their consciousness.[14] The
earth was considered a home for sacred forces and
the origin of all forms of life. The early Greeks were

aware that Earth had a power *(physis)* that encompassed land and sky. This power transcended space and time and was the ultimate ground of reality, unfolding like a flower and giving birth to the world. The medieval person was more interested in the quality of Earth than its quantity: Earth was perceived more as an organism than a machine, and was understood to be the intersection of cosmic purposes and forces, a microcosm within a macrocosm, an embryo within a womb.

If we allow ourselves to follow the path that the ancients took, we will find that God can be hounded through the world's flesh. Since the resurrection of Christ, the deepest faith believes that the Word is present in all things of nature and is always speaking to us of God's nearness and manifestation. In seeing the Word at the heart of physical reality, a reality alive with drama, we feel drawn to a prayer that weaves itself into mountains, seas, and forests and becomes itself a dance.

When I enter the forest I try to concentrate on the mystery of the place. I walk slowly and savor the penetrating silence of Earth, the calm openness of the sky, and the way Earth and sky commune.

I have realized that the response of wonder does not occur automatically; it has to be developed through a love for Earth and a willingness to delight in the sheer presence of things. Wonder builds slowly through small perceptions: Noticing a blossom, the lean of a tree, the fading light of dusk—these accumulate until the landscape is transformed into something more and finds its way into the heart.

"What we lack," says Abraham Heschel, "is not a will to believe but a will to wonder."[15] A life without wonder is a life of monotony, the dull thud of repetition in our ears. There are days when we wake up without hope, spirits dulled by schedules and the ugliness of human selfishness. Yet, retain a sense of wonder and you retain an awareness of the mystery of life that allows you to see beyond schedules and human failings.

Sometimes, though, the world seems closed and common, as if its resources are exhausted, and there is nothing more to see. According to an ancient bit of Hebrew folklore, an angel recites the Torah to a newborn child, passing on all the knowledge the child will need. Afterward, the angel places a finger on the child's lip, forming a cleft, and says one word, "Forget." Who has not felt that at one time or another we were told a story about mystery, a story that we sometimes remember in snatches as if awaking from a deep sleep? Our intuitions of reality, the sense of our deepest self, our relationship with the natural world, are the stuff of dreams which we snatch from an angel on occasion.

Jacob dreamed of angels descending and ascending a ladder and sharing the breath of life as they passed. He heard God's promise that the land he slept on was holy, a gateway to the divine. Isaiah

heard the angels announce "Holy, holy, holy is Yaw-
eh Sabaoth. His glory fills the whole earth" (Isaiah
6:3). Angels are messengers of hope and love, and of
God's earthly presence. They bear the light of leaves
and trees and fill our hearts with sunsets and sunrises. Harboring these angels in our memory allows us
to live in the conviction that we can draw close to
God in the world.

Yet, this is not the whole story. "Every angel is ter-
rifying,"[16] writes Rainer Rilke in the opening lines of
the *Duino Elegies*. Angels may bear witness to a higher
level of reality but too much reality can become aw-
ful. Have you ever encountered beauty in nature that
was so overwhelming that it was terrible or frightening? Have you ever, for example, felt the calmness of
a lake or ocean at dusk when its clarity and stillness
seemed awesome in its independence and power?
There is nothing to do but stand in shock and avert
the eyes. We may know and love angels who call us
to the invisible, says Rilke, but we fear that we may
lose our existence to the invisible world and so we
cling to the security of the visible.

Even if we have little direct experience of these
messengers of divinity, we have faith that the world
is always alive with beauty and love in its depths: It
constantly overflows with goodness. Why? Because
the Spirit of God roams through the world, penetrating its depths and preventing it from falling into pri-
meval nothingness. The fading beauty of a landscape
at dusk is always revived in the light of day. God is

no abstract presence but the warmth of love knitted through the human breast and through the heart of the universe. To believe in this, even if we do not see it all the time, is cause not only for wonder but for ecstasy.

Amazed, we ask with Abraham Heschel, "Who lit the wonder before our eyes and the wonder of our eyes? Who struck the lightning in the minds and scorched us with an imperative of being overawed by the holy as unquenchable as the sight of the stars?"[17] Wonder is a gift, a grace, a subtle movement of the heart that allows us to intuit the depths of nature and the secret resources of our own spiritual lives. Through wonder, Heschel reminds us, we discover our indebtedness, the ultimate realization of the self and the world as sheer gift we did nothing to deserve.

Wonder is not limited to ways of seeing the world because it is primarily a way of being alive. Vision is important, but even more important is the heart's vulnerability toward mystery.

It would startle some people to find how prayerful-wonder is more readily found in the writings of naturalists than in books on religion or the spiritual life. It is impossible, for example, to read the journals of Henry David Thoreau or John Muir without feeling a need to turn to God in adoration. Listen to Muir's description of camping among the sequoias: "When I entered this sublime wilderness the day was nearly done, the trees with rosy, glowing countenances seemed to be hushed and thoughtful, as if waiting in conscious religious dependence on the sun, and one naturally walked softly and awe-stricken among them."[18]

Even naturalists like Loren Eiseley and Annie Dillard, whose close scrutiny of the planet may at times leave us feeling hardened and indifferent toward nature, astonish us with their compassionate interest in everything in the universe, and their deep capacity for wonder. Annie Dillard's observations of the natural world, for example, uncover randomness, terror, and violence, but this is not the whole story:

> I return from one walk knowing where the killdeer nests in the field by the creek and the hour the laurel blooms. I return from the same walk a day later scarcely knowing my own name. Litanies hum in my ears; my tongue flaps in my mouth, "*Ailinon*, alleluia." I cannot cause light; the most I can do is try to put myself in the path of its beam....the secret of seeing is to sail on solar wind. Hone and spread your spirit till you yourself are a sail, whetted, translucent, broadside to the merest puff.[19]

Wonder spontaneously overflows into prayers of gratitude. Thankfulness is not complicated but immediate and simple. Watch the subtleties of light and color when early morning shadows recede; proclaim the immensity of the universe as you stare at the night sky—and you risk dropping to your knees, applauding the magnificence of creation. Francis of Assisi was known to take such great joy in contemplating nature that he danced through the countryside throwing out his arms in praise and thanksgiving.

Who has not walked though the woods on a spring day, smelling the sweet smell of the forest and basking in the glow of sunlight, and not felt the need to pirouette or fling arms into open space? Prayer is a response to soft light in the foliage and thick, moist earth underfoot; it is a spontaneous, joyful worship of being alive and feeling completely rejuvenated. No words can suffice; we dance like King David whirling before the ark of the covenant or Francis spellbound along a country path. D.H. Lawrence tells us, "We ought to dance with rapture that we should be alive and in the flesh, and part of the living, incarnate cosmos."[20]

4

Learning to Bow

Every being has its own interior, its self, its mystery, its numinous aspect. To deprive any being of this sacred quality is to disrupt the larger order of the universe. Reverence will be total or it will not be at all.

Thomas Berry

In one of her essays Annie Dillard tells of a neighbor who was attempting to teach a stone, "a palm-sized oval beach cobble," to talk.[1] Most people, she says, respect his work, which, so far as anyone can imagine—no one has seen the ritual—involves taking the leather-wrapped stone off a shelf several times a day. She suspects the effort includes dedication and self-sacrifice, freeing the person to become an open channel for the work.

Learning to appreciate the intricacies (and voices)

of a flower, a tree, or even a rock may be the first step in learning reverence. "All created things are God's speech," writes Eckhart. "The being of a stone speaks and manifests the same as does my mouth about God...."[2] Jesus himself said: "If [my disciples] were to keep silence, I tell you the very stones would cry out" (Luke 19:40). A great Chinese Buddhist thinker, Dosho, retired to the desert when his intuition that every being, even stones, possessed Buddha-nature was rejected by his contemporaries. There he discoursed to the masses of rock and found them nodding to him in agreement.[3]

The relationship between stone and the human spirit can be traced to early myth where primordial people believed that the core of the earth was rock, an absolute reality, and was capable of bearing all forms of life, including the human race. Perhaps borrowing on the dynamic power of this mythical image the Israelites cried out, "O Lord, my rock and my redeemer" (Psalm 19:15).

Today we may find listening to stones confusing, yet we are at a point in human history where we are once again able to appreciate the mystery of elemental matter. Theoretical physics has re-introduced us to knowledge that mystics of all religions have had for a long time: Life can rise from matter that seems cold and dead, that stones, composed of a mysterious subatomic world of matter, heat up, breathe, and even communicate.

However, reverence for an insignificant thing such

as a stone takes work. We cannot settle for an occasional acknowledgment that the world is sacred but we need an ongoing realization of our indebtedness to God for a world charged with drama and divinity. We need to grow in our reverence toward nature, pulling the stone off the shelf several times each day, enjoying it, protecting it, nourishing its influence on our hearts, as Annie Dillard's neighbor was said to have done. Rainer Rilke imagined that Michelangelo caressed the unhewn surfaces of stone, listening carefully before he made his first cut with the chisel.[4] More recently, sculptor Constantine Brancusi addressed stone with ecstatic reverence while polishing it, immersing himself in a primal world where matter becomes mystery, a locus of the sacred.

This compassionate reverence toward nature seems like a response that is unconnected to the more important realities of human relationships and human desires. After all, how does reverence for an insignificant thing like a stone lead to love for another human being or even affect the fear that may surround our own death?

A short story by Carson McCullers describes an encounter between a young paperboy and a drunken man in an all-night diner. The drunk shows the boy a picture of his wife who left him fifteen years ago to run off with another man. He goes on to tell the boy that in those days he knew nothing about love. Through the years and his mistakes, he developed a philosophy of love. He said that his greatest failure

came when he attempted to love a human being before he learned to love the small things in his life.
This new philosophy, he explains to the boy, is first
to love a rock, then a cloud, and then a tree. Soon
your power to love will increase and you will know
what it means to love a woman.

In another example, a poem entitled "Meditations
of an Old Woman,"[5] Theodore Roethke captures the
poignant drama of a woman who, in the last years of
her life, has lost hope:

> It is difficult to say all things are well,
> When the worst is about to arrive....

Yet, even though she is unwilling to see a shining
future, the woman learns to simply wait without fear.
Through her unguarded waiting she learns to listen to
small things like a "snail's music,"

> And the far phoebe, singing
> The long plaintive notes floating down...

In the face of death she discovers security and spiritual balance, since "birds are around" and "stones
can still be caressed." She finds wisdom in these insignificant events and begins to hear a speech that issues from a power within and beyond all the things
and creatures of this world. Her death becomes less
imposing as she discovers that "I become the wind"
and "recover my tenderness by long looking."

While waiting for the end, she learns compassion

for the small things in nature and for the memories of her past. Withstanding suffering and feelings of loss, she finds she has not been deserted by divine power; eternity has broken through time and offered her comfort. Through her love and reverence for the insignificant she sees infinity in birds and stones and, bearing witness to a world alive with grace, uncovers strength to continue waiting in the darkest of times.

"We live on the fringe of reality and hardly know how to reach the core," says Abraham Heschel.[6] What inspired the authors of Job, Ecclesiastes, and the Psalms if not a world of mystery, capable at any time of revealing God? Reverence felt in the presence of the natural world is a response to the divinity concealed in nature. God is found in the depths of stars and in molecules, and is the ultimate force in roses and whales. Each and every cell bears the divine imprint. Realizing that God is everywhere present—this is where reverence begins.

Native Americans gazed out at the land and called it sacred—even if the land were windswept and barren. Brave Buffalo of Standing Rock, a member of the Oglala Sioux, came to this awareness early in life: "When I was ten years of age," he recalls, "I looked at the land and the rivers, the sky above and the animals around me, and could not fail to realize that they were made by some great power. I was so anxious to understand this power that I questioned the trees and the bushes."[7] Those who would consider this comment an expression of simple pantheism forget that it reflects the same holistic vision that is shared by mystics and great teachers of all religions.

Each thing in nature holds a secret and its existence is the unfolding of this secret under the watchful, loving attention of God. Like the light of noon, God radiates through us and through the natural world, giving grace to all life. This awareness does not cause us to worship nature but to realize that the whole universe is sacred and that we are part of the universe. To revere nature is to revere ourselves because human beings and nature, though not the same, are also not different.

A sense of reverence can be uncovered close at hand in daily events like the enjoyment of food. Instead of pushing food into our mouths while absorbed in conversation, we begin to concentrate on what we are eating and appreciate its giftedness. In one of their ceremonies the Navajos take corn pollen and place it on their tongues, give some to the earth, and then offer the rest to the sky—the stars and the sun. This entire ritual is a way of giving thanks for the blessings of Earth even before prayer begins.

Plants growing inside the house call forth reverence because we tend to see them as mystery, as growth that is not controlled by us, only nourished. Native Americans thanked plants and animals and hesitated to remove rocks unnecessarily from what was considered their proper places. Prayers were said daily for the blessings of sun, air, and water.

What would happen if the lakes and underground streams were so contaminated that we no longer could depend on them for water? "Suppose the sun were extinguished: or the sea were dry," suggests Thomas Traherne. "There would be no light, no beauty, no warmth, no good fruits, no flowers, no pleasant gardens....Prize it now you have it, at any rate, and you shall be a grateful creature: more than this you shall be a divine and heavenly person. ...not to prize them is to be in hell."[8]

It is difficult for us today to imagine the radical relationship with nature that can develop through reverence. We have grown accustomed to intellectualizing both the land and animals and have subsequently lost contact with both. In his study of the behavior of wolves, *Of Wolves and Men,* Barry Lopez suggests that breaking through the intellectual screen is possible by entering natural landscapes and experiencing firsthand both the land and the vital presence of animals.[9]

While following a path along the side of a mountain one afternoon in early spring, I passed beneath a large rock outcropping, turned the corner, and found myself face to face with a whitetailed doe. She froze in her tracks and her wide eyes locked on me. Everything was magic for a moment, but then she took a few steps backward, turned, and leaped through the brush. The spell was broken. I saw only a thread of brown bobbing and weaving through space. The encounter itself awakened me to the inextricable link between animals and humans. Though the doe did not speak nor have a depth of consciousness, she was somehow related to my world and I felt her presence. For a second or two the encounter stripped away the usual way of seeing deer and heightened my perception of the mystery of the animal.

Laurens Van der Post tells of an experience he had while shooting a film on the natural world of Africa. He encountered a rhinoceros and watched it for days, cautiously following the animal whenever their paths crossed. One day he found the rhino in a clearing and decided to approach, unafraid that the animal might charge, feeling only that the rhino wanted the encounter as well. This is his description of the meeting:

> I stood there for about two or three minutes looking at him and wondering about him. I thought with great emotion how beautiful he was....I found nothing that, in the context of its time and the language of life, was not dignified, honorable, and exceedingly lovely. I have not often been so moved by such a sense of discovery as he gave and this new capacity of response he evoked within myself; this resolution that once you break through into the rhinoceros's idiom, discover what a rhinoceros mother would find beautiful in a rhinoceros son, the impression animal beauty makes on you is blinding. All these emotions went through me while looking at him, until there came a moment

when he turned sideways. He said a sort of
"goodbye" and I too turned away.[10]

This kind of encounter with an animal is what the
poet Rainer Rilke calls in-seeing, an almost godlike
perception.[11] It does not mean looking within an animal to see what it has to offer the human world; it
means moving into the center of an animal's being,
that very place where it is most unique, where God
can be found dwelling and taking pleasure, as it
were, in the existence of this particular creature. Such
seeing is not for the timid; whoever encounters unexpected mystery and holiness in another being is certainly changed in the process. What is sacred in the
human recognizes what is sacred in the animal, and
the encounter creates its own mysterious power.

Recognizing the awesome sacredness at the center
of an animal's existence allowed Native Americans to
see that animals could give meaning to human lives.
To take the name of an animal, for example, meant to
take on its power. Joseph Epes Brown quotes Black
Elk: "One should pay attention to even the smallest
crawling creature, for these too may have a valuable
lesson to teach us, and even the smallest ant may
wish to communicate with a man."[12] This reverence
for creatures and the lessons they teach us are also
found in the book of Job:

If you would learn more, ask the cattle,
seek information from the birds of the air.

The creeping things of earth will give you lessons,
and the fishes of the sea will tell you all.
There is not one such creature but will know
this state of things is all of God's own making.
He holds in his power the soul of every living
thing,
and the breath of each person's body (12:7–10).

In his commentary on Genesis, Walter Brueggemann explains that "dominion" (from the phrase "subdue...and have dominion" [Genesis 1:28]) is similar to the dominance of a shepherd over sheep.[13] It refers to the responsibility of looking after the well-being of creatures by tending and feeding them. It does not mean the exploitation of the land nor animals. He adds that the appropriate model is Jesus, who saw that his responsibility of lordship included servanthood, the willingness to lay down his life for his sheep. Dominion, then, means a responsibility for creation's well-being and enhancement so that it truly lives up to its purpose as God's creation.

Who could represent this model of servanthood toward creation more ideally than Francis of Assisi, the saint who embraced the gospels with his entire being and who showed respect and compassion even for earthworms and reptiles? Francis's love and care for nature came from the deepest posture of his heart, namely, his sense of indebtedness to God which he discovered through his poverty and humility. He emptied himself so completely in imitation of the poverty of Christ that he experienced the fullness of both nature and God.

His joyous sense of unity with the world resounded in his reverent address to animals and elements as brother and sister. According to one story, Francis received a bird as a present from a nobleman and addressed it as "brother pheasant." The bird responded to Francis, as did many creatures, by refusing to leave him even when it was set loose in the wild.

In his biography of Francis, St. Bonaventure writes that the saint possessed an "abundant piety" toward creatures.[14] The Latin word *pietas* has a broader context than our popular notion of pious; it includes meanings such as love, kindness, and reverence. Also, *pietas* was a Roman virtue that referred to the preservation of family life and the need for reverence for the family structure to exist. Using this word in reference to the saint, St. Bonaventure seems to be emphasizing Francis's compassionate relationship with nature as well as his willingness to include in the family matrix all the natural world, extending into the universe itself.

Francis's profound reverence for creation is dramatically represented in the famous fresco by Giotto, *Francis Preaching to the Birds,* in the Upper Basilica in Assisi. The artist depicts the saint bowing humbly, the posture of a true servant, before all creation while exhorting the birds to praise God. The compassionate heart of this bowed figure overflows with the fullness of God's creative love, which he sees reflected in the world around him. It is not difficult to imagine Francis and the birds offering praise to God. The birds were like wild angels that found a refuge in his soul and repeatedly called him homeward.

Reverence for the created world is surely a mark of sanctity. A saint is willing to explore the depths of humanness, to nurture the wellspring of passion and love in the soul so that love flows from every pore and life, and to extend the self fully and compassionately into the world. A saint is poor in spirit, battling against false pride and learning to forget the self, knowing that this is the way of unity and love. Those, like Francis, who lose themselves for the sake of love follow the way of the servant and gain the fullness of the world.

An uncanny parallel to Francis can be found in Chuang Tzu. Just as Francis preached profound poverty and humility so that the heart could find a place for Christ, Chuang Tzu talked of an essential humility in which a person's heart is emptied in order to accommodate the indwelling of the Tao:

> The man in whom Tao
> Acts without impediment
> Harms no other being
> By his actions
> Yet he does not know himself
> To be "kind," to be "gentle."[15]

In both men the path of humility led to an all-embracing response to living things, a humble communion with all living creatures. They both possessed a vision of a primordial paradise where humans could live in peace with each other and with all creation.

As saints and great teachers testify, reverence is never simple; it quickly places a person in a dilemma. Preserving one life we often sacrifice another; going out of our way to show respect for the dignity of one creature, we trample another without thinking.

Albert Schweitzer, whose "reverence for life" is the ethic of love widened into a universal context, would be the first to admit that reverence is not an easy path to follow. He once bought a young, crippled fish eagle from African natives in order to save its life.[16] He had to decide whether to let the eagle starve to death or to kill several small fish a day to keep it alive. He opted for the latter course but became aware of the difficulty that arises when someone tries to assist life and avert suffering. In preserving one life another is often lost in the bargain.

In a sermon on reverence for animals, Schweitzer reflects on killing a large spider which he knows will spin its web and torture many insects; why let this pain occur in the world, why not stop it?[17] He concludes that there is no universal solution to the problem; every situation is different. So long as we act with a sense of responsibility and according to conscience, says Schweitzer, our actions are justified.

Above all, we should concentrate not on taking life but on preserving it.

Should we take the opportunity to save an insect helplessly flailing about in a pool of water or a worm that has strayed onto a sidewalk? The important thing, according to Schweitzer, is to act when our conscience prods us to do so, and in acting we will discover what it means to be a human being. We must retain our humaneness by preserving, as best we can, the dignity of life. The naturalist Loren Eiseley, reflecting on his own capacity for empathy, agrees with Schweitzer's position:

> No, it is not because I am filled with obscure guilt that I step gently over, and not upon, an autumn cricket. It is not because of guilt that I refuse to shoot the last osprey from her nest in the tide marsh. I possess empathy.... I share that sympathy and compassion which extends beyond the barriers of class and race and form until it partakes of the universal whole. I am not ashamed to profess this emotion, nor will I call it a pathology. Only through this experience many times repeated and enhanced do we become truly human.[18]

If it is true that "not a sparrow is forgotten before God" (Luke 12:6), then we must be assured of God's attention not only to humans but to every buzzing particle of the universe. How amazing and incomprehensible it is to imagine a God who cares for all things, for molecules and galaxies, who is involved in the life of each human being and in the remote corners of the universe! It was Julian of Norwich's insight, while examining a hazelnut in the palm of her hand, that all life is so fragile and delicate that it needs to be held in existence by God's love.

Whoever realizes the divine creativity in the physical world, intuits the sheer "giveness" of things in all their variety and fecundity, their splendor and grace, may suddenly be overwhelmed by the nearness of the holy. Response at times like these is not the normal prayer of thanksgiving said in polite tones but an indescribable need to bow that comes from the center of one's being. This gesture is devoid of forethought; an immediate, spontaneous response to the nearness of God in the world, a response of deep humility in the face of mystery.

You can never bow often enough when you are aware of how gifted life is. Consider this description of a walk that writer and naturalist Barry Lopez took while camped in the western Brooks Range of Alaska:

> I took to bowing on these evening walks. I would bow slightly with my hands in my pockets toward the birds and the evidence of life in their nests, because of their fecundity, unexpected in this remote region, and because of the

serene arctic light that came down over the land
like breath, like breathing.[19]

Reverence engages us deep in the natural world. It
offers access to a divine core of the world, taking our
relationship with nature out of the arena of easy sen-
timent and anchoring it in humility before God.

As I walk a forest path I become more conscious of
breathing and have the sensation of sweet air rushing
into my lungs, expanding my chest, and flowing out,
moist and warm, into the landscape. Every breath increases participation in the forest. The molecules of
air are shared by hawks and maple trees, a snorting
buck, and a meandering mountain stream. The air
that hums in my ears as I rush down the side of a hill
blew through the tops of trees, was whipped into a
frenzy by storms, and lingered in the cool valley at
night. I breathe with the forest and let its breath pass
through me.

I realize that I do not live on Earth but in relationship with it. According to a Navajo poem, the lines
on my fingers are "the tracks of wind."[20] Hebrews
talked of *ruach* and *nepash*, the life-breath of all
things. Each breath mingles with the heart, pulses
through the arteries, and flows out to include the energy of the world. Each breath is a blessing, a mark of
holiness both for one's being and for the world. As I
walk, a deep reverence for the breath of God grows
within me, a humble primary response to the Spirit
that flows through all reality.

What changes occur to us when we encounter nature with reverence? Faith certainly deepens through contact with a God who is so near. Also, our very lives are transformed; learning reverence for nature, we learn it for our own being. We are struck by the holiness and love of God and our lives are consecrated. "They who keep holy the things that are holy shall themselves become holy," writes Abraham Heschel.[21]

5

Listening to the Silence

A night in which the silence was audible,
I hear the unspeakable.

Henry David Thoreau

Thomas Merton, who uncovered the ways of nature's silence in the beautiful Kentucky landscape, offers this insight in the preface to the Japanese edition of *Thoughts in Solitude:*

No writing on the solitary, meditative dimensions of life can say anything that has not already been said better by the wind in the pine trees. These pages seek nothing more than to echo the silence and peace that is "heard" when the rain wanders freely among the hills and forests.[1]

Merton's deep appreciation of nature's silence and its relationship to his spirituality and prayer became obvious to me during a conference on the monk's theology, writings, and life. The culminating event of four days of programs and talks took place at Merton's hermitage, the place where he spent the last years of his life. About two hundred people sat on bales of hay surrounding the small cement-block cabin and listened to Ron Seitz, a poet-friend of Merton, recite the monk's poetry. Hearing these poems read, one after the other, seemed to have a transforming effect on the people gathered together on this unassuming knoll in late May.

One poem in particular, "In Silence," had a dramatic effect on the listeners. As the words were read I imagined Merton rocking in a chair by the fireplace, reading, reflecting, praying, and intermittently looking out over this seemingly tame Kentucky landscape.

Be still
Listen to the stones of the wall.
Be silent, they try
To speak your
Name.
Listen
To the living walls.
Who are you? Whose
Silence are you?

Who (be quiet)
Are you (as these stones
Are quiet). Do not
Think of what you are
Still less of
What you may one day be.
Rather
Be what you are (but who?) be
The unthinkable one
You do not know.

O be still, while
You are still alive,
And all things live around you
Speaking (I do not hear)
To your own being,
Speaking by the Unknown
That is in you and in themselves.
I will try, like them
To be my own silence:
And this is difficult. The whole
World is secretly on fire. The stones
Burn, even the stones
They burn me. How can a man be still or
Listen to all things burning? How can he dare
To sit with them when
All their silence
Is on fire?[2]

At the last lines of the poem, a gasp rose from the

audience. Suddenly this plain Kentucky hillside, where all had seemed common and peaceful, was alive with the silence of nature and the silence of human solitude. We witnessed for a brief moment the fire that Merton saw flaming in these hills.

Merton was well acquainted with silence. His monastic life was lived in silence and his prayer entered the depths of contemplative silence. Few are aware, however, of the continuous and powerful influence that the silence of the landscape had on his prayer. From the early days of monastery living, Merton's journals were filled with talk of nature's silence. Around the time of his solemn profession he wrote: "This afternoon I was content looking at the low green rampart of woods that divides us from the rest of the universe and listening to the deep silence...."[3]

Early on, he recognized that the silence of the woods can become a source of life for the spirit and can offer the soul harmony and grace. Silence has a way not only of calming the mind but of opening the heart. Inner life begins to flow freely and concentration intensifies. Ultimately, Merton realized that this rich, provocative silence throughout nature is woven into our lives, that it is not a thing outside us but an ineffable presence that calls us to prayer. Reveling in the effects of silence, he writes, "...my chief joy is to escape to the attic of the garden house and the little broken window that looks out over the valley. There in the silence I love the green grass. The tortured gestures of the apple trees have become part of my prayer."[4]

When he turned fifty, Merton thought he was ready for real solitude. Since he was allowed to spend more and more time in the hermitage built on a knoll just above the monastery complex, he grew enormously in his appreciation of his life and the landscape. He delighted in the solitary expedition, happy with waking in the hermitage, with hearing rain in the trees, and especially with experiencing prayer alone in the silence of nature and God's presence: "...it is the place God has given me after so much prayer and longing and without my deserving it, and it is a delight. I can imagine no other joy on earth than to have such a place to be at peace in. To live in silence, to think and write, to listen to the wind and to all the voices of the wood...."[5]

In the physical and spiritual environment provided by the hermitage, Merton celebrates the sheer existence of being alive in the woods, the absolute lightness of being, and promises himself: "a solitude in which one allows nature this virginal silence, this secret, pure, unrelatable consciousness in oneself."[6]

Merton's relationship with nature's silence heightens our own awareness of how easily the calming atmosphere of a forest or the stillness of a lake at dusk can lead us into prayer.

Our experience of prayer in the silence of nature commonly begins in small, simple ways and not in

dramatic ones. At one time or another we have experienced a mysterious silence in our wanderings
through a landscape: a walk through the woods in
winter, the shock of desert stillness, listening to
waves at the shore—all of these introduce the depth
of nature's silence. Recalling a walk through the autumn woods, Thoreau writes in his journal: "The stillness of the woods and fields is remarkable at this season of the year. There is not even the creak of a
cricket to be heard."[7]

I stop in the woods and no longer hear my footfall
or the sound of my breathing, and the large silence
presses in. Especially when there is a light rain, the
forest stands quiet, immersed in its stillness, no
breath of wind, no birdsong, no animal rummaging
in the brush—and I am overwhelmed by the silence.
Unfamiliar with this silence one feels unsettled, want-
ing something—anything—to happen.

In time I began to realize how intimately the silence of nature is related to the human spirit. There
was nothing special about the silence of the woods
until I allowed myself to encounter it—then, it became dramatic. The silence that I normally thought
was separate from my life effectively resonated at the
center of my being and intensified prayer.

Philosopher Max Picard, whose writings on silence
influenced Merton, speaks of a profound metaphysi-
cal silence that pervades our existence in ways we
cannot imagine: "The silence of nature presses into
man. The spirit of man is like the sky over the broad

surface of this silence."[8] According to Picard, nature's silence is not passive—it is more powerful than mountains or seas; it is alive, dynamic, an energy at the heart of creation.

Nature's silence can lead human silence to God. By entering the depths of this silence and allowing it to influence our prayer we transform it and discover a path of prayer through nature. This is a common experience for many people who seek out places in nature to pray. The prayer that rises from this silence is no longer ordinary but truly extraordinary, because it touches the mystery of God.

Familiarity with nature's silence may cause us to drop our guard and think of it as predictable or even controllable. This is foolhardy. Describing her encounter with the awesome mystery of silence in a field near a farmhouse she was renting, Annie Dillard writes, "It was the silence of matter caught in the act and embarrassed. There were no cells moving, and yet there were cells. I could see the shape of the land, how it lay holding silence. Its poise and its stillness were unendurable, like the ring of the silence you hear in your skull when you are little...."[9]

An experience like this is unnerving because it reveals a silence that is no longer tame but wild. Furthermore, it is not a gentle, loving silence that we might hope for but one that startles us, shocks us, as if we had put our hand on a hidden source of voltage in nature. This is not the kind of silence you think of controlling but the kind that causes the soul to tremble and call out, "Holy, holy, holy."

There are other experiences of silence, though, where the power is felt, but with less fear and trembling and more appreciation and excitement.

A few summers ago I left a midnight campfire and wandered into a field to see the full moon. The moon, hovering just above the tops of trees, poured light on the landscape. Tall grass and sides of trees were flecked with particles of light. As I stood and stared, the landscape began to hum, and the humming grew louder until the forest resonated with silence. The place was suddenly caught in its own brilliance and overflowed with silence. In a short time the intensity of the light diminished and the silence became less audible. For days, though, I was haunted by the low moon and the buzzing silence.

After experiencing the power of silence you begin to believe that the forms of the natural world float on the broad back of silence and simply respond to its rhythm, that a tree bending and rocking in the wind on a blustery night is simply giving shape to silence. The primacy of nature's silence is essential, says Max Picard. "The silence of nature is the primary reality. The things of nature serve only to make the silence clearly visible."[10] Who could imagine that silence is the womb within which the earth and sky are born?

Nature is truly alive with silence; even the sound of wind in the trees or the plaintive song of a bird seems to issue from the ground of silence. Flowers blossom in silence; trees perpetuate the silence, their sap filled with the quiet rhythm of the earth. Silence rises from the vegetation and flows from dark recesses like a wave; ebbing, flowing, crashing. "The forest," writes Picard, "is like a great reservoir of silence out of which the silence trickles in a thin, slow stream and fills the air with its brightness."[11] Merton offers a fitting prayer: "It is very quiet, O my God. Your moon shines on our hills. Your moonlight shines in my wide-open soul when everything is silent."[12]

Remaining close to the rhythms of nature, attending to sunrises and sunsets or the passage of the seasons, fills one's being with silence. Plants, animals, trees, and streams offer themselves as pools of silence to rest the eyes and draw the heart away from anxiousness toward contemplation. The earth is crammed with silence and silence issues from her pores. Blackberries plump on the vine, under a hot August sun, are bursting with silence.

A person who is centered in this silence becomes tranquil in the same way that a farmer who tills the soil from morning to night feels an overwhelming calmness. One's entire being changes; gestures, speech, vision, and gait all become influenced by the silence. Artificial rhythms are exposed in the pervasive silence and are replaced by natural rhythms that feel more authentic.

This primary silence undercuts artificial, distracting noises that we are usually subjected to in daily life. Going into the deep woods, I find that the weight of silence blankets my being and the human voice sounds lonely and shrill. I begin to whisper and talk only when necessary. I am able to free myself from the chaos of words which I often use to retain the illusion of control. I begin to realize that the words I speak should emerge from deep within the silence and the thought of chatter—talking for the sake of talking—becomes obnoxious.

When silence becomes dynamic and words fail, I am vulnerable enough to listen. Josef Pieper writes:

> ...only the silent hear and those who do not remain silent do not hear. Silence, as it is used in this context does not mean "dumbness" or "noiselessness"; it means more nearly that the soul's power to "answer" to the reality of the world is left undisturbed.[13]

Anyone who spends time in the depths of silence rediscovers the true relationship between words and silence, thoughts and silence, and prayer and silence.

Merton gives a lyrical description of a life lived under the daily influence of nature's silence. While reading this description, think not only of a monk in a hermitage but also a farmer working the fields late in the evening, a beachcomber who stays at the shore from dawn to dusk, or a person on retreat in a desert watching a full moon rise over a canyon. To pray in the silence of nature is

...to deliver oneself up, to hand oneself over, entrust oneself completely to the silence of a wide landscape of woods and hills, or sea, or desert; to sit while the sun comes up over that land and fills its silences with light. To pray and work in the morning and to labor and rest in the afternoon, and to sit still again in meditation in the evening when night falls upon the land and when the silence fills itself with darkness and with stars.[14]

An ancient Chinese compendium for landscape painting, "The Mustard Seed Garden Manual of Painting," advises the painter to "still the heart" in order to enter a deep quietness related to the creative silence of Tao.[15]

Peter Matthiessen describes his spiritual journey through the high snowy mountains of Tibet and the way that the stillness of the mountains, their eternal silence, quickly brought on a state of mind conducive for prayer.[16] He would find meditation spots on rock outcroppings over a hillside and calm his breathing, allowing the silence within to resonate with the silence without. Sometimes amid his prayers he found that the mountains took on life and the blue sky began to "sigh."

As we have seen, the silence that radiates from a thick wood, a forest pond, or a winding creek, has an uncanny way of weaving into the human spirit and opening the heart to unexpected influences. It gives the spirit the impetus it needs to break through the log jam of mental noise and chaos stored up through the business of daily life, and flow freely toward its mysterious source. As a result, spiritual concentration intensifies, and there is an experience of harmony and grace.

Sometimes, though, we enter natural surroundings preoccupied with our concerns, still busy about our lives, and struggle against the influence of silence. However, "The silence of the woods forces you to make a decision which the tensions and artificialities of society may help you evade forever. Do you want to be yourself or don't you?" writes Merton.[17] Remaining in the silence demands a kind of letting go that we may not be prepared for, a willingness to leave behind a restricted vision of self and the world and choose a broader, more truthful stance.

A person who enters nature's silence with the idea of making it into something significant, an expression of one's search for God, for example, will find that the silence becomes inflated with self-importance; it becomes an ego-centered world of illusion, both artificial and false. But those who enter this silence, ready to let go of self-consciousness and the masks that form because of it, will recover a sense of spiritual uniqueness rising from the center of the being, a hidden uniqueness that may have been intuited many times before but was never allowed to flourish.

A person who experiences a new, truthful self, grounded in the mystery of God, knows how neces-

sary it is to continue to live within the realm of silence so that one's existence can become an extension
of silence. Drawing strength from this experience of
silence, it is easier to be yourself during the anxious,
frantic times of daily life; there is no need to try to become someone else. Referring to such a person Merton says, "He does not listen to the ground of being,
but he identifies himself with that ground in which
all being hears and knows itself."[18]

The silence of nature enters your life and becomes
an ineffable presence calling you home. It is not as if
the depths of nature and the depths of the human
spirit were the same, but only that both no longer
stand over against one another and both lean toward
a common ground of silence.

The experience is subtle: Most often it is like entering a clearing, an expansive ground of silence, and
your footsteps carry you deeper into the silence. Or it
is like walking on a wide field that has been blanket-
ed with snow and finding that earth and sky are
transformed into silence. In this clearing, the separation between self and nature diminishes; birds sing
the silence and the song gathers the silence in your
own heart. As in a Japanese *kabuki*, the drama of the
soul is enveloped in fertile silence filled with possibilities of rebirth.

In this silence you come in contact with the unbounded rhythms of the spirit and the need to rein-
force these rhythms and allow them to grow. Rainer

Rilke reminds us, "We must assume our existence as broadly as we can, even the unheard of must be possible in it."[19] Meister Eckhart offers the same view: "Understand now that there is a power in the soul that is wider than the widest heaven, which is so unbelievably wide that we cannot express it."[20]

The awareness of this clearing is a joyful awareness because, drawn by the silence at the depths of nature, we touch on the depths of God's own silence. The silence of God is filled with love and expresses that love through the Word. The experience of silence in this clearing, then, is both creative and joyful. Before long, you learn to lose yourself in the joyful rhythm. In a prose poem entitled "Hagia Sophia," Thomas Merton writes: "There is in all things an inexhaustible sweetness and purity, a silence that is a fount of action and joy. It rises up in wordless gentleness and flows out to me from unseen roots of all created being, welcoming me tenderly, saluting me with indescribable humility."[21]

Remaining in this clearing is not easy because the silence begins to separate us from our preference for the practical and the routine, the normal diversions of life. The mind feels helpless under the sheer weight of silence, and some cannot bear this because they can no longer attach themselves to images and thoughts. Remaining in this clearing, we discover that the silence is truly an entrance into a deeper form of prayer, one that lets go of the ordinary and the mundane and simply rests in God's presence.

Those who cannot tolerate an atmosphere where there is nothing to feed the mind's voracious appetite will flee nature. Those who remain, however, accept the monotony, embrace the silence, and discover that prayer is not self-manufactured but a grace, and that the only thing of importance is the abiding hunger for God's love.

Sometimes the silence intensifies and becomes fire. This is the silence of the burning bush of Abraham and the mountain top of Moses. It is the transforming silence where human faculties of imagination and intellect are useless and we are left facing God with the world around us on fire. Merton writes:

When your tongue is silent, you can rest in the silence of the forest. When your imagination is silent, the forest speaks to you, tells you of its unreality and the Reality of God. But when your mind is silent, then the forest suddenly blazes transparently with the Reality of God....[22]

Both the self and nature become one wick for God's flame. Faith and humility are the only companions in this silence. We burn in the immediacy of God's love and bend our heads low.

It is true that we do not experience the awesome power and depth of silence each time we walk into the woods, wander along the shore, or hike in the desert. Often the silence we encounter is only a state of peace and quiet. The senses become still and the mind grows calm. This state is an entrance into deeper prayer, and often it is the only prayer we have, so we remain and wait.

Sometimes, though, the silence becomes one with prayer so completely that it is transformed into God's own silence. At these times we can say that we go to nature's silence simply because we are drawn by love and find ourselves responding to that love. Merton prays, "Let me seek, then, the gift of silence, and poverty, and solitude, when everything I touch is turned into prayer: where the sky is my prayer, the wind and the trees is my prayer, for God is all in all."[23]

When God's presence fills the silence, we find ourselves in an expanse, a clearing, that is unbelievably wide and anchored in faith and humility. In this clearing we discover union with nature, insight into the ways of the heart, and the immediacy and power of God's love.

How then do you pray in the silence of nature? Go to the landscape that appeals to you, let the silence of the landscape resonate within your being, and let God's presence fill your heart and become prayer. Even if this is not the prayer you anticipate, relax and be at peace with yourself. Say nothing. "Be silent before the Lord God!"(Zephaniah 1:7)

6

A Vision of Light

I saw Eternity the other night
Like a great Ring of pure and endless light,
All calm, as it was bright,
And round beneath it, Time in hours, days, years
Driv'n by the spheres
Like a vast shadow mov'd, in which the world
And all her train were hurl'd.

Henry Vaughan, "The World"

I once stayed at a cottage in northern Canada, a place
I had sought out for the kind of prayer and solitude
that is nourished by living close to nature, day by
day, for a long period of time. The cottage rested on a
large rock and overlooked a wide and beautiful bay,
which in turn was surrounded by dense forests of

pine, spruce, and cedar. During the day the blue-green water and the bluish cast of the sky mirrored each other and charged the atmosphere. At night, the sky opened into a brilliant expanse of dancing light. The landscape was overwhelming and I felt my vision graced.

Early one morning, after several months at the cottage, I looked over the bay and watched the islands roll like ships in waves of mist. Then, suddenly, I experienced a deep sense of warmth and peace. I realized that everything was shining with an indescribable light, the rocks, water, and especially the white pines at my side. The entire bay shimmered and opened before me, full and inviting. I felt like those who dream of a strange land, only to wake and discover that they were home all the while.

Again and again, during the year-long stay at the cottage, I learned that seeing cannot be controlled; it is a grace of awareness that originates in the deepest part of the being. You see nature in a divine light, a light that at the same time you witness within yourself.

In his biography of St. Francis of Assisi, G.K. Chesterton describes a time when Francis entered a cave and underwent a radical transformation. Chesterton says that Francis entered the cave with one view of the world and left with another: He went in seeing as an ordinary person would see and came out with the eye of a fool.[1] This foolish perspective was due to his unique vision of a world completely dependent on

God. For most people at the time, the visible was the
primary basis for seeing; for Francis, the invisible was
the founding reality. The focus of Francis's eyes was
a world immersed in and flowing from the dynamic
light of God's presence.

"Seize God in all things,"[2] says Meister Eckhart. To
see in this way is to see with an intense awareness of
the concrete and particular, and especially with the
overwhelming certainty that all things are embraced
by God. It is necessary to see not mystery in the
world, but the world in mystery.

This kind of seeing is risky because it awakens a
love for the world and a call to deeper faith. The eye
grows hungry and the soul seeks transformation. The
light of the heart reflects the light of nature: Light resonates with light. Bede Griffiths relates the following
experience, which happened during a period of conversion:

> I had come through the darkness into a world of
> light. ...it was as though I had been given a new
> power of vision. Everything seemed to lose its
> hardness and rigidity and to become alive. ...the
> hard casing of exterior reality seemed to have
> been broken through, and everything disclosed
> its inner being. The buses in the street seemed to
> have lost their solidity and to be glowing with
> light.[3]

Moses was tending his father-in-law's flock in the

Sinai Desert when fire flamed from an ordinary bush. When Moses approached the burning bush in wonder, God called out from the bush, "Moses! Moses!" He answered, "Here I am." God said, "Come no nearer! Remove the sandals from your feet, for the place where you stand is holy ground" (Exodus 3:4–5). Later in his life, Moses participated fully in this divine light. When he descended from the mountain of Sinai, having spoken with God, his face was so radiant that his followers backed away from him and would not come close until he called them.

During her desert wanderings, Israel herself was led by the light of a pillar of fire. When the world goes up in flame, what more can you do but recite your name and follow the brilliance, marking the ground sacred as you go? Seeing puts your entire being at stake, and God addresses you in a way that you least expect.

Didn't Jacob Boehme catch a glint off a piece of pewter and hold it in his inner eye so that it would become a beacon reminding him of God's nearness? And shouldn't each one of us catch the flash of light in our eye, let our souls become a lightning rod, and walk around with a vision of the burning nearness of God? Jesus' voice constantly challenged those who have eyes to see and ears to hear. Who can see that the kingdom of God is nowhere but here, now? Grace is alive in our own backyard!

I came across the surprising story of Jacques Lus-

seyran.[4] Blinded by an accident at school when he
was eight, Lusseyran remained blind for thirty-seven
years of his life. Even though the light that illuminat-
ed objects was no longer available, he began to discover an inner light. It was a great revelation for him
to discover that the source of light was not outside but
within. The character of this light was amazing, since
it seemed to have infinite resources, and constantly
spilled out into the world. Like other blind people, he
found that he had a difficult time finding his way
among objects, but soon discovered that when he began to depend on this inner light for guidance, he
was able to avoid accidents. As soon as he forgot it,
however, he was at risk again.

Another insight he had was that the inner light
was related to his capacity for love. When love was
weakened through anger, envy, sadness, or hate, the
light diminished and he felt truly blind; the dimensions of his universe began to shrink and his inner vision was severely limited. Yet, when he was in touch
with love, he felt abundant joy, space opened again,
and the world became a realm of infinite possibilities.

Francis of Assisi himself composed "The Canticle
of Brother Sun" when he was almost totally blind and
unable to see the beauty of the world. Yet, his words
praise creation like no others. Though struck blind by
an eye infection, he depended on the light of his own
soul, which radiated through his entire body and
gave him a sense of unity with creation. Confidence
in this light through a lifetime of dedication to it ena-

bled him to write an extraordinary song about the beauty of the natural world.

The spiritually enlightened are represented as bathed in light; they also irradiate light which is depicted by an aura around the heads of saints and *bodhisattvas* in Christian and Buddhist art. It is light that originates within and suffuses the body, extending outward into the world.

The awareness of light in our own experience, even for a brief time, offers insight into the depths of the human spirit far beneath the surface of immediate experience. We discover the integration of the inner and the outer, of the self and the world.

The perception of light, states Boethius, is "the greatest of all pleasures, since sight is but the harmonious meeting of two types of light, that of the physical world and that of consciousness."[5] Furthermore, "Light is the purest essence that exists, the most sublime beauty, the object whose presence causes the greatest joy."[6] St. Augustine and St. Bonaventure would agree with Plotinus who wrote in the *Enneads:* "The fullest life is the fullest love, and the love comes from the celestial light which streams forth from the Absolute One."[7] This idea is at the same time Greek, Oriental, and medieval. It is also biblical. God is at once luminous and incandescent:

...the King of kings and the Lord of lords
who alone is immortal,
whose home is in inaccessible light,

whom no man has seen and no man is able to
see...(1 Timothy 6:15–16).

In the New Testament the desire to see is at the
same time an awakening hunger for Christ. A blind
man made his way through the crowd and approached Jesus. "Jesus asked him, 'What do you want
me to do for you?' 'Rabbi,' the blind man said, 'I
want to see'"(Mark 10:51). Each of us hungers to see,
hungers for a contemplative vision in which we discover Christ who proclaims, "I am the Light of the
World" (John 8:12).

Jesus fulfilled the Old Testament prophecy that the
people would be healed of their blindness:

But I will make the blind walk along the road
and lead them along paths.
I will turn darkness into light before them
and rocky places into level tracks.
...Look and see, you blind! (Isaiah 42:16–18)

This hunger to see the light of God everywhere
draws us into the depths of creation in response to an
ultimate craving. If the eye is filled with light and not
with darkness then we go freely, not blind to the
grace that God offers us in the world and in our own
hearts. Light resonates with light. The Spirit moves
without and within, heightening our awareness of
the Word in all things.

Taking a closer look at the lilies of the field, as

Francis of Assisi did, we may find that their splendor captures us completely and opens us to an understanding of the gospel. In the lilies Francis found a love for the created world rooted in gospel poverty. God speaks in simple visions if we have eyes to see. The disciples on the way to Emmaus did not recognize their companion but "their eyes were opened." Later, he vanished, leaving them with their vision (Luke 24:31).

It is common knowledge that lovers see with the greatest longing. The fulfillment of this longing can be found hidden in the natural world. If we allow ourselves to see beyond the ordinary, and nurture the desire to see deeply, God's presence will become abundant and the world will appear sacramental. This seeing, however, is a risk; it can catch us off guard and become a transforming hunger, an insatiable desire to see more, which never ceases and which we crave for the rest of our days.

A person seized by the light of the Spirit may want to exclaim with St. Symeon in the *New Theologian:*

> I share in the light, I participate in the glory,
> and my face shines like my Beloved's,
> and all my members become bearers of light.[8]

Usually, however, our seeing is only surface perception, a way of orienting ourselves in space. The eye moves over the surfaces of people and landscape and there is no depth, only appearance. We see this way habitually, out of daily necessity; but this kind of seeing is too quick and too utilitarian to evolve into prayer. Of all our senses, sight is the weakest. We need to deepen our sense of sight through concentration or, a better word, attention. Then we may begin to see God in many things; tadpoles, water, even snakes and dragonflies.

The gentle eye goes deeper than the prodding eye. Reality can appear radiant to the eye that is open to contemplative seeing. When the eye is captured by the infusion of light it seeks the source, and the heart expands and grows.

Referring to attention in an essay on school studies, Simone Weil says that it is not the result of willpower, grinding teeth, and knitted brow, but has its origin in deep desire, and is nurtured in an atmosphere of joy.[9] Attention certainly involves effort, but it is a *negative effort*, not the obvious effort of forcing ourselves upon an object, but the more subtle effort of remaining detached and empty, ready to participate and receive the imprint of the object.

Attention means a long, hard look at something but with the kind of concentration that allows this particular lichen-covered stone, its color shifting from a green to a bluish cast, to impress itself on the heart, and lead us into the present, into the very center of the event.

Attention means watching buds, bundles of leaf and blossom compacted into a sheath, begin as small beads glistening in the new light of spring, then break into time. Their process is elusive to the casual eye, but for one who looks attentively, they become the focus of a landscape as they sit on an April branch tightly furled and ready to blossom like a hand uncurling.

I have a favorite meditation spot at the top of a hill about a mile from the place where I often camp. Whenever I go there in the early morning, I position myself on the back of a fallen tree so that I can watch the first streams of light flood the horizon and crease the heads of the maples, oaks, and pines. These wave-like rhythms of light transform the landscape and hint at the infinite. Whenever I see this show, I imagine it is happening for the first time, my vision awakening from a primal darkness.

Looking at the forest in this way, I see not so much an outline of things but a flash of light pulsating; trees, for example, are patches of color straining to emerge from the darkness. This seeing holds my attention so completely that I forget myself and feel bound to the landscape, intensely aware of the vital nearness of things: water, soil, air. I sit for a long time in the shimmering landscape, adrift in the heave and swell of morning light.

In one of his sermons Meister Eckhart refers to the arrival of light as the "birthing" of all things from their source. Earth shines forth; flowers, stones, woods, and hills radiate. Through this unbounded light the world is constantly renewed and my vision is charged.

Through attention, a person—most often in a subtle way—experiences what it means to forget separation between self and nature and feel a common bond with the world. According to Evelyn Underhill:

Nature herself reveals little of her secret to those who only look and listen with the outward eye and ear. The condition of all valid seeing and hearing, upon every plane of consciousness, lies not in the sharpening of the sense, but in a peculiar attitude of the whole personality: in a self-forgetting attentiveness, a profound concentration, a self-merging, which operates a real communion between the seer and the seen—in a word, in contemplation.[10]

You watch the movement of a bird, weaving through the air, seemingly suspended in the sky, displaying its own incredible grace. You let your eyes rest on the bird floating overhead, not projecting your emotions but accepting its uniqueness and beauty as these are given. You find that natural perception deepens and becomes contemplative—a prayer.

This was the vision of Gerard Manley Hopkins who lost himself in the movement of a falcon riding the currents of air that rolled beneath its wings. He expressed his vision in a poem, "The Windhover," which has no religious symbolism but is dedicated to Christ, the Word, who is the uniqueness within all things. Through this poem Hopkins shows us that there is no need to make natural perception into something religious; it becomes religious in itself the more we are able to appreciate the individual quality of ospreys, whales, horses, and falcons. We encounter the Word whenever we become lost in a creature's beauty and individuality.

It is helpful to study artists in order to find new ways of seeing the world, since our own ways often seem so inadequate. An artist possesses an ease of seeing that escapes most people. Whoever would learn to see as an artist should realize that the eye must be connected to the heart so that vision can be guided by love. An artist chooses to create out of love for seeing, not out of love for technique.

Discussing the artist's ability to create, Robert Henri writes that "It is harder to see than it is to express."[11] The first time Georgia O'Keeffe visited Taos, New Mexico, she was immediately attracted to the highlands. The vast scale of the land, its lonely mountains and overwhelming skyscape, intensified her vision and exhilarated her spirit. She took many walks and drives, exploring the area, allowing the landscape to call forth images from her psyche which she later used as the bases for her paintings.

O'Keeffe was quick to recognize that the barren landscape and its mysterious, pure light had qualities that integrated her personality on an unconscious level, and gave her a unique and penetrating vision of the natural world. She began to see the simple forms and vibrant colors of flowers and hills; this is what she would eventually paint.

Claude Monet watched the rising sun drench the landscape, prized the way this first light modified tones and shades, and revealed the texture of haystacks. He painted several variations of a haystack. Each painting is a little different not only because of perspective but also because of the glance of light. Looking at several of these paintings in one room, a viewer realizes quickly that the quality of light changes the texture and mood of these paintings so dramatically that, in one instance, a particular haystack is so tangible you can feel it; and, in another instance, it is so ephemeral that it threatens to disappear into a mystical haze.

Complete attention to a natural object may reach a point where the ego becomes unusually porous and there is pure receptivity; only the object exists, empathetically perceived, as it were, from within. The result is a prayer where the mind sheds its separation from nature and an identification with mystery is possible.

Several years ago, I was camping along Little Salmon Creek and eating breakfast. After I finished breakfast I retrieved water from the creek to wash a pot and some utensils, all the while preoccupied with thoughts of the day ahead.

As I leaned over to draw water, my attention became riveted on points of sunlight dancing on the creek. The light mesmerized me and I let my whole attention focus on it. Suddenly, the landscape began to change. Water, trees, rocks, and ground drew near, so near that I felt the surface of a large boulder on the opposite side of the creek as if it were next to my skin. The surface felt porous and smooth; at the same time, it appeared translucent, a physical presence that became an aperture into something hidden.

I stood in a daze. The whole place shimmered with a radiance I had not seen before. What joy! I felt the intimate presence of things and intuited with certainty that all nature was loved and cared for. I was also aware of the love that pulsed at the center of my being and felt regret for having ignored it for so long. I was overwhelmed by the realization of how dependent I was on this love and how near it was to my life. A deep sense of humility filled my heart, and I was overcome by the indescribable need to bow low before the mystery of nature and the sacredness of my own being.

The joy reached a crescendo and suddenly abated. The awareness of mystery and love was replaced by the sense of a threatening abyss. My life felt as if it were on the edge of the abyss and could be lost at any moment; nature herself seemed fragile and derelict; emptiness overwhelmed the entire event. Slowly, though, the abyss receded. I was left shaken but with a deep reassurance that, as fragile and dependent as all being is, it would still be held in existence by love.

After a time (I am not sure how long a time it was), the landscape withdrew and knitted itself tight. Water, rocks, trees, and earth collected themselves as if someone were rearranging stage scenery. The landscape that remained had all the familiar distances. The sound of rushing water, in particular, was so clear and intense that it seemed removed from the senses.

All things returned to concealment. The points of light continued to dance but there was no longer any depth; the rhythm had vanished. The only song that remained was the one still singing in my heart.

Long after the emotion had waned and I had left the forest, I realized that I could no longer be content with ordinary seeing in which I took my life for granted. My sight had been changed and so had my heart. I wanted to celebrate nature, to address all things in a way that I had not done before—from the depths of my being—and I wanted to celebrate the mystery of a call, a call to transform my life in love. I realized, too, that I no longer had to search for an image of home but that I was already home and had not known it. Mystery was nearer to my life than I had thought; my life was immersed in it.

When the *I* becomes porous to the surrounding world, a person becomes involved in a vibrant, un-centered perceptual field, a mystery. This awareness of light is not ordinary awareness; it is a state of grace. Our lives and the world are in a tenuous state,

constantly filled to the brim and ready to flow over—
and we hardly notice.

However, nothing much comes of an encounter
with light without some commitment. Once the contour of the ego fades, a spiritual process needs to begin, a surrender to a higher law, a willingness to answer the grace of deeper prayer. Seeing means little
and leads nowhere unless there is faith and a commitment to the spiritual life—this is the counsel we receive from the desert fathers and mothers and holy
men and women through the ages. Ongoing surrender to God's will is necessary to contemplate the creative love imminent in all things.

Evagrius of Ponticus, a desert father himself, di-
vided the spiritual journey into three stages: *praktike,
physike,* and *theologia.* In the first stage, *praktike,* a person learns to practice virtue and find a certain peace
in the struggle to overcome the dark side of the self.
The next stage, *physike,* is a form of natural contemplation in which one is able to see created reality as it
exists in God. The final state, *theologia,* is contemplation of God as God and knowledge of the Trinity.

According to these stages, it is apparent that Evagrius thought a prayerful relationship with the world
was possible only after a person, through the practice
of the virtues, realized some degree of freedom from
the pull of desire. A sign that a person was ready to
move into the stage called *physike* or natural contemplation is "...when the spirit begins to see its own
light..."[12] Other signs were the ability to pray without

overwhelming distraction and the awareness of the powers that reside in the soul. Only when these signs are present, according to Evagrius, can the world be seen as it truly exists—in God.

Thomas Merton, influenced by his study of Evagrius, also emphasized the need for natural contemplation in the growth of the spiritual life, and insisted that it be accompanied by a certain purity of heart. Merton felt strongly that natural contemplation, a prayer we do not hear much about today, is a necessary stage for those interested in a serious commitment to the spiritual life and that it is "inseparable from love and from a truly spiritual conduct of life."[13]

Whose life could be a better model for natural contemplation than that of Pierre Teilhard de Chardin? Teilhard not only loved the world but took seriously the purity of heart necessary to embrace it: "To be pure of heart means to love God above all things and at the same time to see him everywhere in all things."[14] Purity of heart, for Teilhard, was the result of purification, concentration, and great moral effort. Hearing the deeper call of nature, he responded with a passionate embrace of the diaphanous, luminous oneness of all things. In relationship with this all-embracing unity, he realized that he himself "had become pure light."[15] His vocation afterward was to give witness to this light that he saw at the center of his being and at the heart of the universe.

Attention, as we have seen, engages the physical

world in a kind of dance. Instead of trying hard to see
something, you allow your eye to admire and enjoy,
to learn the steps of the dance. You let go of your control and allow nature to lead you. You learn to look
with a quiet, receptive eye, with the eye of a lover,
and you begin to feel the rhythm.

Walk alone, unhurried, and let your eyes rest on a
boulder, a branch, or a leaf; the web of a spider, the
texture of bark—the things that attract your attention.

Photographer Alfred Steiglitz would lie on the
ground and gaze at the sky watching clouds pass
overhead, continually forming and reforming themselves into different shapes. Watching the movement
of this tenuous substance triggered Steiglitz's imagination. When the formations drifting across the sky
reflected his emotions, he raised his camera and took
a picture. By eyeing the "cloudscape" he harvested
the images of his own heart.

Looking at the stars at night, the soul lights up and
the music rises. In the city you barely notice the stars;
in the wide expanse of an open country field you
can't take your eyes off them. Black space stippled
with tiny points of light whispers of distant galaxies
and mysterious worlds. The constellations loom overhead and overpower the darkness; they track across
the sky, causing the mind and the eye to move in a
curve.

Your eyes flash with the pulsing sky and refuse to
quit. You try to look away but find that the light has
stitched itself into your brain. Going to sleep, you en-

vision shooting stars and the blanketing, incandescent sky.

The night sky is glory; it is the story of God's handiwork. Returning to it refreshes our memory and restores a sense of humility before the vast mystery of the universe. The brilliance provides unusual comfort and balances our dreams. Francis of Assisi, drawn by the brightness and splendor of the moon and stars wrote in "The Canticle of Brother Sun": "Praised be you, my Lord, for Sister Moon and the stars; You have formed them in heaven clear and precious and beautiful."

It is important to realize, though, that nothing is automatic. Light is not always revealed to us; most of the time it remains concealed. However, for the believer, revelation is present even when it is not witnessed directly. We live in the potency of revelation. We live at the center of light, even if we are not always aware of what this means.

Jesus addressed two blind men and asked if they believed in a cure. They said, "'Sir, we do.' Jesus touched their eyes and said, 'Your faith deserves it, so let this be done for you.' And their sight returned" (Matthew 9:27–30). "The man who has God essentially present to him grasps God divinely, and to him God shines in all things," declares Meister Eckhart.[16]

7

The Forest at Night:
A Song of Praise

Acclaim God, all the earth,
play music to the glory of God's name....

Psalm 66:1,2

Night arrives slowly in the forest; daylight yields to deep, quiet darkness. As the darkness grows, it penetrates the soul and renews it. I walk in this stilled world, among the trees and the shadows, and feel the nearness of the earth; there is no distance, only thoughts of kinship. The forest is silent and accepting, reminding me of God's fertile, intimate presence. This is a time of poetry, of standing in wonder and awe at the dream that flows through nature and through my being.

There is still light in the sky and the maple trees are radiant witnesses; darkness may be collecting at their feet but they catch the last rays on their crowns in a moment of glory. Fireflies have begun their dance in the tall grass of a small field, weaving a flashing tapestry under a gunmetal-gray sky. I rest in the magical transformation of the forest and think of praise.

In the previous chapters we found our way into the heart of nature through silence and light. Now, hearts awake to the nearness of the holy; we discover a prayer of praise.

Walking through a landscape, our consciousness blazing with the heat of God's nearness, what can we do but praise? The entire earth is filled with the glory of God. Praise is a primary response to this glory which we are graced to see. "My heart sways with the world," exclaims Theodore Roethke. "I am that final thing,/a man learning to sing."[1]

Praise may only seem like a simple reflex reaction to God's presence, but it is much more. It is a way of giving thanks for a graced existence that we suddenly realize is ours. Praise opens up the heart, makes our life a conduit; recognizing how much we have been given, we are eager to extend our gift to others. Praise is also an acknowledgment of the awesome hunger we have for divine love. Love is the word hidden at the center of praise because ultimately praise is nothing more than a spontaneous, graced act of love for God. What greater prayer is there than simple praise?

It is easy to think that praising God in and through nature is too difficult and that other prayers, like prayers of petition, are simpler and make more sense.

Yet, a prayer of praise is more primary than a plea for help in time of need. Praise does not originate with practical concerns but rises spontaneously from a heart filled with joy. The psalmist praises God out of the sheer joy of being alive: "Praise the Lord, O my soul!" (Psalm 104:1).

The vibrancy and spontaneity of the psalms as shouts of praise are lost to us today because we see the completed, fixed form of the psalm and forget that this was only a final stage in the process of development. In fact, the psalm of praise began with a short cry, "Praised be God..." by a person who encountered the nearness of the divine. This single sentence originally stood as an independent verbal unit to which other elements were later added.

At this simple level of a spontaneous cry, it is easy to imagine the psalm as a primary prayer that gathered power from somewhere within a person and was expressed in language that was immediate and direct. These singular cries from the depths of one's being are the origin of authentic praise and are found at the root of every religious experience.

Any time we pause in wonder and awe at the mystery of nature or our own being, we may discover the exclamation, "O Lord!" issuing from our mouths. Having been moved deeply, we evoke God's name without thinking and praise fills our being. The Israelites traced the experience of joy to God, for it was in God that all joy originated. All things were created fundamentally good according to the Genesis story, and praise is the response to this goodness as well as its reaffirmation.

Praise is not a prayer that aspires to rise above the world; there is no inclination to leave behind the finite for the infinite. It does not use nature as a platform to catapult into the heavens but is rooted firmly in the earth with the belief that it is within the earth that we find divinity. God's love is not hidden behind creation but bodied forth in the presence of each form that appears before us, even the small and insignificant.

When St. Patrick was sent to Ireland as a bishop he was confronted by a multi-cultured society headed by kings and tribal chieftains. These people, representing widely diverse traditions, asked Patrick what his God could offer them. This was the saint's reply:

Our God is the God of all . . . the God of Heaven and Earth, of sea and river, of sun and moon and stars, of the lofty mountain and the lowly valley; the God above Heaven, the God in Heaven, the God under Heaven; He has his dwelling round Heaven and Earth and sea and all that in them is. He inspires all, he quickens all, he dominates all, he sustains all....[2]

In his answer Patrick readily describes a God who embraces heaven and earth in divine intimacy. As a result, in Celtic Ireland you find a holy relationship between tilling the soil and the spiritual journey. Patrick's religion was adaptable to an ancient nature worship, yet it preserved the power of a transcendent God. In the eyes of anchorites and monks who founded hermitages and monasteries on wild hillsides and rocky promontories, nature was transparent; the universe was sacramental, a vibrant sign of holiness—and an occasion for praise.

Once we become aware of the activity of God in the world, then our own relationship with the earth can be understood as an involvement in God's own interest. In focusing on God's love, which is near to us, we participate in God's creativity. Through our prayer of praise, for example, we join God in proclaiming the goodness of the earth and, in so doing, help to shape both her destiny and our own.

We realize God has a stake in this physical reality through the Incarnate Word. When we pray the Apostles Creed we acknowledge the union of heaven and earth through the incarnation. How can we offer praise unless we believe that the incarnation is alive and well today in our lives? Is Christ truly coursing through our veins; is he the unity who holds all things together: the salty seas, the thick forest, the motion of the planets? Owen Barfield contends that the proof of our belief in the incarnation will be evident not when it becomes an issue in theology journals but "when it becomes impossible to write a popular manual of science without referring to the incarnation of the Word."[3]

We take the entire world with us in our prayer to the Lord. All things participate in the incarnation. Even the travesties of the environment—the destructive power of storms, earthquakes, and volcanoes—bear witness to it in their own way.

Francis saw Christ's face in the terror of the natural world as well as in the beauty. When he walked through the countryside he envisioned the imprint of the cross everywhere. He did not simply imagine the image of the cross superimposed on the surface of the world, but saw the suffering and chaos at the heart of matter.

Describing a meeting with an ascetic one day on Mount Athos, Nikos Kazantakis writes:

He was holding a poplar leaf up to the light and looking at it, the tears flowing from his eyes. Surprised, I stopped and asked him, "What do you see in that leaf, holy Father, that makes you cry?"

"I see Christ crucified," he answered. Then he turned the leaf over and his face beamed with joy.

"What do you see now that makes you so happy?" I asked him this time.

"I see Christ resurrected, my child."[4]

If God is truly "all in all," says Merton, then everything is ultimately paradise because everything is filled with the glory and presence of God.[5] In fact, we are never separate from God but only think we are because of our blindness. Because we are prodigal sons and daughters, our perception is limited. When we break away from the blindness, through self-giving and humble openness, we will discover a new vision of ourselves and the world and will truly celebrate the resurrection.

The world is sacramental and the pathways we discover through it are filled with bushes that explode into flame and streams that dance with light. At times this love may reveal itself, flame out, and we return home beating our breasts. Christ hides in the thick of the flesh and in the heart of nature. The world is holy and we do not have to go to the desert to see it.

Sitting on the side of a mountain, I watch the sun glide down over a range of hills and recite a verse from the psalms: "Acclaim God, all the earth, play music to the glory of God's name..." (Psalm 66:1,2). As I repeat the words, they rise full-throated from the depths of my being and vibrate in the silence. The forest turns to darkness and the last light is reflected on the back of Little Salmon Creek, a silver slip of ribbon winding through the shadows below.

To recover the spirit of the psalms you need to rest in nature and allow it to nurture your soul; you need to sense the presence of what is hidden and hear voices ringing in the stars and stones. Then, one day, you will realize that matter is open and the day manifests

God. You will stare at the mute forest and watch the distant stars and suddenly become aware of the murmuring of matter, the burgeoning voice that rises from the center of cells. Praise erupts from the heart unexpectedly, straining toward language; to praise is to discover one's voice directed toward God.

Because the psalms are not rational discourse but poetry, they have the power to open a passageway into the heart of creation. The psalmist sees goodness and responds with metaphor rather than reflection, with celebration rather than description. "The creature's proper mode of speech about creation," declares Brueggemann, "is not description but lyric, not argumentation but poetry."[6]

> You crown the year with your bounty,
> abundance flows wherever you pass;
> the desert pastures overflow,
> the hillsides are wrapped in joy,
> the meadows are dressed flocks,
> the valleys are clothed in wheat,
> what shouts of joy, what singing! (Psalm 65:12–14)

As poetry, the psalms move beyond the limitations of literal language and explore the dimensions of God's presence in history and nature, which dimensions defy human comprehension. Also, as poetry, the psalms introduce us to a world where things exist not in isolation but in relationship. Poetry best expresses, through its use of metaphor, the hidden energy connecting things. In the mind of the psalmist, earth, air, water, birds, and people are somehow related, and the language of poetry allows this relationship to reveal itself.

Poetic metaphors only work, however, if we bring to them the fullness of our experience and a free association of ideas. When we do this, we strip images of their ordinary character and allow them to explode into a fireworks of meaning displaying a surprising array of depth and nuance. Contemplating the summer sky on the slope of a hill, for example, we might expand our vision by thinking of the view of the sky from an airplane or from a spaceship, or imagine planet Earth, small and fragile, journeying through the infinite expanse of the universe. Then we read:

The heavens proclaim your glory, O God,
and the firmament shows forth the work of your hands;
day carries the news to day,
and night brings the message to night (Psalm 19).

More importantly, poetic expression parallels God's activity in bringing the world into existence through speech; "God said, 'Let the waters under the heaven come together...'" (Genesis 1:9). It is through speech that creation comes into being, and it is through speech that God and creation are bound together in a relationship that moves toward the fullness of time when unity and harmony will be complete. "We know that the whole creation has been groaning in travail together until now; and not only creation, but we ourselves" (Romans 8:22,23).

As the expression of God, all parts of nature are poetry since they are the word that God speaks and continues to speak. It is apparent, then, that poetic words are much more than a particular style of expression; they indicate to us that nature participates in divine revelation. Poetry draws us into participation with all reality spoken into being by God. Through the spontaneous praise of the psalms we discover a sense of kinship with streams, mountains, and hills, and find a path to the one who spoke the primary Word.

Our praise of God reminds us that we are not isolated from nature but that we are at home, in unity with the natural world. Nature is not a cold piece of matter separate from our spiritual lives but is filled with God's spirit and shares our spiritual destiny. In the depths of our prayer we discover that we "wait with eager longing" (Romans 8:19) not alone, but with all of creation.

Because we live in a secular culture centered on human will, we imagine that our purposes are independent of God's purposes. It is no wonder that we ignore a wider vision that would include God's will for creation. "The tragedy of modern man is that he thinks alone," writes Abraham Heschel. "He broods about his own affairs rather than thinking for all being. He has moved out of the realm of God's creation into the realm of man's manipulation."[7]

There is a complex interplay between our salvation and nature. Since nature is created by God, it will always surprise us and leap beyond our imagination. We may sometimes take our environment for granted and try to manipulate it, but we are really in over our heads. When we admit that we cannot know the mystery of the natural world, then we may be more willing to see that our own spiritual journey back to God, with both its suffering and joy, is connected with the journey of the whole universe back to the Creator who made it and who alone can bring it to completion.

Paradoxically, our very sense of isolation from nature creates a desire for a spiritual relationship with her. Our alienation triggers a profound, unconscious need to find a unifying love in the world and to affirm the earth in a way that is deeply prayerful.

The spiritual journey of the Christian community cannot take place without the companionship of nature and without integrating her into the process. This has been the message of teachers throughout history, such as St. Paul, Irenaeus, and Francis of Assisi. It is not only the body that is raised at the end of time but the entire physical reality. This world is not an accidental creation. God has a purpose and continues to re-create the world toward that purpose out of love.

It is up to us not to ignore Earth nor flee from her.

We cannot forget our connection with humanity but, also, we cannot forget our connection with Earth. As pilgrims, we are not alone but are bound to heaven and Earth. Otherwise the words of the creed in which we proclaim one God, "maker of heaven and Earth and of all things visible and invisible," lose their meaning.

Our prayer and spiritual life should reflect our deep spiritual kinship with nature. Since the world itself holds a divine mystery, to address nature, as St. Francis knew, was to address God; and to affirm the value of nature is to affirm the value of one's own existence. No matter how distant nature seems to us or how little emotion we may feel toward her, our spiritual life is intimately related to the world of creation, and we know this with certainty in our deepest prayer.

Awakening to our common destiny with creation, we may suddenly become aware that the physical world is not a quiet partner but conspires to open us to the divine meaning inherent in our lives and the potential of our own spirituality. Since creation herself is oriented toward God, she reinforces this orientation in us. The longing of our own heart is echoed in the yearning of the natural world. Creation teaches us in her own wise way about spiritual matters; she is a guide, a companion on the spiritual journey, and leads us back to God.

Those who encounter divinity in nature and discover a prayer of praise filling their hearts also find that nature herself is filled with alleluias. Nikos Kazantakis offers his own experience:

> Listening intently, I heard the spirit which stands by every blade of grass to help it grow and accomplish its duty on earth. Here in my impregnable solitude I sensed that even the most insignificant of God's creatures—a grain of wheat, a worm, an ant—suddenly recalls its divine origin, is possessed by a God-inspired mania, and wishes to mount step by step in order to touch the Lord; the wheat, worm, or ant to touch Him and stand at His side along with angels and archangels, it too an angel, an archangel.[8]

Nature invites us to a chorus of praise where even the stones speak and the the heavens answer with light. Every single thing is an ode of joy since it is the focus of God's love and reflects that love. What is it like to allow our prayer to merge with the praise of creation? The Celtic saint, Columba, wistfully imagines:

> Delightful would it be to me to be in Uchd Ailiun
> On the pinnacle of a rock,
> That I might often see
> The face of the ocean;
> That I might see its heaving waves

Over the wide ocean,
When they chant music to their Father
Upon the world's course....[9]

The psalms, in particular, reveal praise echoing in
every molecule: "The heavens declare your glory, O
God, and the firmament shows forth the work of
your hands" (Psalm 19:2–3). There is nothing left to
do but praise God in the company of all nature. In the
words of Abraham Heschel, "Man is not alone in celebrating God. To praise Him is to join all things in
their song to Him. Our kinship with nature is a kinship of praise."[10]

Praise God, sun and moon,
praise God, shining stars,
praise God, highest heavens,
and waters above the heavens!
Let them all praise the name of God,
at whose command they were created (Psalm
148:3–5).

Not only the light side of creation is called to
praise but the dark side as well. All that is frightening
or seems evil to us, all that escapes human comprehension praises God:

Praise the Lord from the earth.
you monsters and all deeps,
fire and hail, snow and mist,

stormy wind fulfilling his word! (Psalm 148:7,8)

Extending praise to include all creation is difficult for us to accept today. It seems like a superficial gesture, or so much imaginative rhetoric. Yet, if we believe in the fundamental goodness of creation as the psalmist did, then we have a relationship with creation that serves as ground for our praise. Singing the song of the earth, we sing the song of God. We should describe ourselves as beings "...in whom this grand diversity of the universe celebrates itself in conscious self-awareness."[11] Praise engages us in a harmony that flows through the world. The world is alive, molecule by molecule, and joins with our prayer of joy, laughter, and celebration. Kazantakis heard this short poem on Mount Athos: "Sister Almond Tree, speak to me of God. And the Almond Tree blossomed."[12]

By its very being, its unfolding, a tree tells of the glory of God. Nothing is heard, no speech, no information, only the glorification of God. This proclamation is an event that never ceases. We watch the rising and the setting of the sun, the ongoing occurrence of night following day, and we discover the story of God's glory that has been told from the beginning of time.

Night is approaching, and I watch the valley grow thick with shadow. Before fading, light balances for a short time with the darkness. This is not really a gray time but a time when colors grow mute and distant, calm, and reticent. The rich green of the foliage passes through subtle shades and textures; the trees are no longer thick and heavy but ragged and ghostlike. Darkness increases and as the landscape disappears the cool scent of damp earth rises.

I begin a fire along the bank of the creek and sit in the dark nurturing the flames. The cool air fills with pockets of heat and I huddle close. Doors that close in light swing open in the dark. The gurgling sound of the creek becomes more distinct; the sound reaches a crescendo, then breaks apart, scattering. In the darkness, boundaries recede and the sound sifts through my being; the flow without joins the flow within. In the night I become more visible to myself than in the light. I cannot think of sleep; my whole being is awake and loud with reality.

I sit with my attention immersed in the fire, occasionally looking up at the night sky and watching the brilliant display of starlight. Fire charms; light becomes a dream. Staring into the fire, I realize that I am not the one who perpetuates the dream of my life, but that I am dreamed. The light is a metamorphosis of the soul opening it to its own love and the love that flows throughout nature. In the flood of light, tenderness enters the heart, gently and subtly uncovering an enormous compassion for all beings.

When I surrender to this flame as I am doing tonight, it becomes the source of peace and life. I go to the woods to be in the presence of this original flame, this flame at the center of creation and at the center of my own being. This is an epiphany of the heart; it is all I know and all I wish to know.

Epilogue

As I leave the forest and Little Salmon Creek behind and return to the activity of daily life, I take a dream with me, a dream of mystery and of divine presence that has woven itself through streams, woods, deer, and sky and through the center of my being. Even when my attention is focused on some activity, the dream continues to unfold in my unconscious, healing my spirit and calling me toward a deeper commitment to the spiritual adventure.

On occasion, the dream world rises full force and I stand in awe before the depth of the world around me and the hidden dimensions of my own inner life. Most of the time, though, I simply remember the prayer that evolved in the forest, along Little Salmon Creek, and allow it to fill my imagination and wake my spirit.

I hope this book has afforded some small access to this dream for others who find themselves wondering at a world too mysterious for human comprehension and who realize that we cannot fully mine the resources of our own spiritualities without first discovering—and celebrating—the hidden dimensions of the natural world.

Notes

1. At the Side of Little Salmon Creek

1. Quoted in D.T. Suzuki, *Zen Buddhism*, ed. William Barrett (New York: Doubleday Anchor, 1956), p. 251.

2. *Ibid.*

3. *Heidegger: The Man and the Thinker*, ed. Thomas Sheehan (Chicago: Precedent Publishing, 1981), p. 27.

4. May Sarton, *Journal of a Solitude* (New York: W.W. Norton, 1973), p. 16.

5. Thomas Merton, *Conjectures of a Guilty Bystander* (New York: Image Books, 1968), p. 294.

6. *Heidegger: The Man and the Thinker*, p. 28.

7. Quoted in Margaret Smith, *The Way of the Mystics: The Early Christian Mystics and the Rise of the Sufis* (New York: Oxford University Press, 1978), p. 63.

8. Jacob Boehme, *The Signature of All Things* (Greenwood, S.C.: The Attic Press, 1969), p. 91.

9. Thomas of Celano, *Saint Francis of Assisi*, tran. Placid Hermann, O.F.M. (Chicago: Franciscan Herald Press, 1963), p. 72.

10. *The Heart of Thoreau's Journals*, ed. Odell Shepard (New York: Dover Publications, 1961), p. 133.

11. Thomas Merton, *Contemplation in a World of Action* (New York: Image Books, 1973), p. 258.

12. Margaret R. Miles, *Practicing Christianity: Critical Perspectives for an Embodied Spirituality* (New York: Crossroad, 1988), p. 177.

13. *Ibid.*, p. 180.

14. *Celtic Christianity*, ed. Christopher Bamford and William Parker March (Massachusetts: Lindisfarne Press, 1987), p. 33.

15. Rudolph Otto, *Mysticism East and West: A Comparative Analysis of the Nature of Mysticism,* tran. Bertha L. Bracey and Richenda C. Payne (New York: Macmillan Publishing, 1976), pp. 58-59.

16. *The Heart of Thoreau's Journals*, p. 119.

17. Mary Collins, *Women at Prayer*, 1987 Madeleva Lecture in Spirituality (Mahwah, N.J.: Paulist Press, 1987), p. 26.

18. Quoted in Evelyn Underhill, *Mysticism* (New York: E.P. Dutton, 1961), p. 58.

2. Awakening to the Call of Beauty

1. Quoted in Claudio Naranjo and Robert E. Ornstein, *On the Psychology of Meditation* (New York: Viking Press, 1971), p. 91.

2. Kenneth Clark, *Landscape Painting* (New York: Charles Scribner's Sons, 1950), p. 7.

3. For a discussion of the change in St. Augustine's thought on creation see H. Paul Santmire, *The Travail of Nature: The Ambiguous Ecological Promise of Christian Theology* (Philadelphia: Fortress Press, 1985), pp. 55-73.

4. *Bonaventure: The Soul's Journey Into God; The Tree of Life; The Life of St. Francis,* tran. Ewert Cousins, *The Classics of Western Spirituality* (New York: Paulist Press, 1978), pp. 67-68.

5. *Journal of a Solitude*, p. 123.

6. *The Asian Journal of Thomas Merton,* ed. Naomi Burton, Brother Patrick Hart and James Laughlin (New York: New Directions, 1975), p. 234.

7. Rollo May, *My Quest for Beauty* (New York: Saybrook Publishing, 1985).

8. Bede Griffiths, *The Golden String: An Autobiography*

(Springfield, Ill.: Templegate Publishers, 1980), p. 10.

9. *Ibid.*, p. 108.

10. It has been suggested that the Irish tradition, more specifically, the Irish *peregrini* who wandered the countryside evangelizing, were models for the Franciscans, who also saw themselves as pilgrims and strangers living and teaching the gospel. See Edward A. Armstrong, *Saint Francis: Nature Mystic* (Berkeley: University of California Press, 1976), pp. 34-41.

11. Matthew Fox, *Breakthrough: Meister Eckhart's Creation Spirituality in New Translation* (New York: Image Books, 1980), p. 121.

12. *A Hopkins Reader*, ed. John Pick (New York: Image Books, 1966), p. 67.

13. *The Wilderness World of John Muir*, ed. Edwin Way Teale (Boston: Houghton Mifflin Company, 1976), p. 100.

14. Wendell Berry, *Recollected Essays 1965-1980*, "An Entrance to the Woods" (San Francisco: North Point Press, 1981), p. 236.

15. *Meister Eckhart: The Essential Sermons, Commentaries, Treaties, and Defense*, tran. Edmund Colledge, O.S.A. and Bernard McGinn (New York: Paulist Press, 1981), p. 205.

16. Eloi Leclerc, O.F.M., *The Canticle of Creatures: Symbols of Union* (Chicago: Franciscan Herald Press, 1966), p. 65.

17. *A Hopkins Reader*, p. 51.

18. Loren Eisley, *Night Country* (New York: Charles Scribner's Sons, 1971), p. 173.

19. *The Confessions of St. Augustine*, tran. John K. Ryan (New York: Image Books, 1960), p. 113.

20. *St. Francis of Assisi*, p. 270.

21. *The Confessions of St. Augustine*, p. 254.

3. Waiting for Dawn

1. *The Home Planet*, ed. Kevin W. Kelly (New York: Addi-

son-Wesley Publishing, 1988), p. 107.

2. John Shea, *Stories of God: An Unauthorized Biography* (Chicago: Thomas More Press, 1978), p. 16.

3. *The Collected Poems of Dylan Thomas* (New York: New Directions, 1957), p. 178.

4. Antoine de Saint Exupéry, *Wind, Sand and Stars*, tran. Lewis Galantiere (New York: A Harvest Book, 1967), pp. 76-77.

5. *The Heart of Thoreau's Journals*, p. 45.

6. *A Hopkins Reader*, p. 47.

7. *Ansel Adams: Letters and Images, 1916–1984* (Boston: Little, Brown and Company, 1988), p. 125.

8. Theodore Roethke, *The Collected Poems of Theodore Roethke* (New York: Doubleday, 1975), p. 236.

9. Freeman Dyson, *Infinite in All Directions* (New York: Perennial Library, 1989), p. 7.

10. Laurens Van der Post, *A Walk with a White Bushman* (New York: William Morrow and Company, 1986), p. 31.

11. Abraham Joshua Heschel, *Man Is Not Alone: A Philosophy of Religion* (New York: Farrar, Straus and Giroux, 1976), p. 76.

12. Thomas Merton, *New Seeds of Contemplation* (New York: New Directions, 1961), pp. 296-297.

13. James Lovelock, *Gaia: A New Look at Life on Earth* (New York: Oxford University Press, 1979).

14. Mircea Eliade, *The Sacred and the Profane* (New York: Harper & Row, 1961), p. 12.

15. Abraham Joshua Heschel, *God in Search of Man: A Philosophy of Judaism* (New York: Farrar, Straus and Giroux, 1976), p. 46.

16. *The Selected Poetry of Rainer Maria Rilke*, ed. and tran. Stephen Mitchell (New York: Vintage Books, 1984), p. 151.

17. *Man Is Not Alone*, p. 68.

18. *The Wilderness World of John Muir*, p. 217.

19. Annie Dillard, *Pilgrim at Tinker Creek* (New York:

Bantam Books, 1975), p. 35.

20. D.H. Lawrence, *Apocalypse* (Aldington: Penguin Books, 1974), p. 126.

4. Learning to Bow

1. Annie Dillard, *Teaching a Stone to Talk: Expeditions and Encounters* (New York: Harper & Row, 1982), p. 67.

2. *Meister Eckhart: The Essential Sermons, Commentaries, Treaties, and Defense*, p. 205.

3. *Zen Buddhism*, p. 247.

4. Rainer Maria Rilke, *Stories of God* (New York: W.W. Norton and Co., 1932), pp. 115-21.

5. *The Collected Poems of Theodore Roethke*, pp. 151–165.

6. *God in Search of Man*, p. 56.

7. Joseph Epes Brown, "The Bison and the Moth: Lakota Correspondences," in *Parabola*, Vol. VIII, No. 2, p. 6.

8. Thomas Traherne, *Centuries, Poems and Thanksgiving*, Vol. 1, ed. H.M. Margoliouth (London: Oxford University Press, 1958), p. 23.

9. Barry Lopez, *Of Wolves and Men* (Toronto: J.M. Dent and Sons, 1978).

10. *A Walk with a White Bushman*, p. 17.

11. *The Selected Poetry of Rainer Maria Rilke*, p. 313.

12. "The Bison and the Moth: Lakota Correspondences," p. 97.

13. Walter Brueggemann, *Genesis: A Bible Commentary for Teaching and Preaching* (Atlanta: John Knox Press, 1982), p. 32.

14. *Bonaventure: The Soul's Journey Into God*, p. 254. I am indebted to Franciscan scholar Dr. Ewert Cousins for his comments on the word *pietas* during a seminar on mysticism at Fordham University.

15. Thomas Merton, *The Way of Chuang Tzu* (New York: New Directions, 1965), p. 91.

16. Albert Schweitzer, *Out of My Life and Thought: An Au-*

tobiography, tran. C.T. Campion (New York: Holt, Rinehart and Winston, 1964), p. 231.

17. Albert Schweitzer, *A Place for Revelation: Sermons on Reverence for Life,* tran. David Larrimore Holland (New York: Macmillan Publishing, 1988), pp. 30-32.

18. *The Lost Notebooks of Loren Eiseley,* ed. Kenneth Huer (Boston: Little, Brown and Company, 1987), p. 155.

19. Barry Lopez, *Arctic Dreams* (New York: Charles Scribner and Sons, 1986), p. 177.

20. Quoted in Peter Matthiessen, "Native Earth," *Parabola,* Vol. VI, No. 1, p. 13.

21. *God in Search of Man,* p. 78.

5. Listening to the Silence

1. *Introductions East and West: The Foreign Prefaces of Thomas Merton,* ed. Robert Daggy (Greensboro, N. C.: Unicorn Press, 1981), p. 91.

2. *The Collected Poems of Thomas Merton* (New York: New Directions, 1977), p. 281.

3. Thomas Merton, *The Sign of Jonas* (New York: Image Books, 1956), p. 69.

4. *The Sign of Jonas,* p. 281.

5. Thomas Merton, *A Vow of Conversation: Journals, 1964–1965,* ed. Naomi Burton Stone (New York: Farrar, Straus and Giroux, 1988), p. 152.

6. *Ibid.,* p. 17.

7. *The Best of Thoreau's Journals,* ed. Carl Bode (Carbondale, Ill.: Southern University Press, 1967), p. 97.

8. Max Picard, *The World of Silence* (South Bend, Ind.: Gateway Editions, 1952), p. 137.

9. *Teaching a Stone to Talk: Expeditions and Encounters,* p. 135.

10. *The World of Silence,* p. 137.

11. *Ibid.,* p. 139.

12. *The Sign of Jonas,* p. 240.

13. Josef Pieper, *Leisure: The Basis of Culture* (New York: Mentor Books, 1963), p. 41.

14. Thomas Merton, *Thoughts in Solitude* (New York: Image Books, 1968), p. 91.

15. Mai-mai Sze, *The Way of Chinese Landscaping Painting: Its Ideas and Technique* (New York: Vintage Books, 1959), p. 118.

16. Peter Matthiessen, *The Snow Leopard* (New York: Bantam Books, 1980), p. 109.

17. *Contemplation in a World of Action*, p. 258.

18. *Introductions East and West: The Foreign Prefaces of Thomas Merton*, p. 91.

19. Rainer Maria Rilke, *Letters to a Young Poet*, tran. M.D. Herter Norton (New York: W.W. Norton and Co., 1962), p. 67.

20. *Breakthrough: Meister Eckhart's Creation Spirituality in New Translation*, p. 126.

21. Thomas Merton, *Emblems of a Season of Fury* (New York: New Directions, 1963), p. 61.

22. *Thoughts in Solitude*, p. 97.

23. *Ibid.*, p. 91.

6. A Vision of Light

1. G.K. Chesterton, *St. Francis of Assisi* (New York: Image Books, 1957), p. 74.

2. *Breakthrough: Meister Eckhart's Creation Spirituality in New Translation*, p. 67.

3. *The Golden String*, p. 107.

4. Jacques Lusseyran, "Blindness; A New Seeing of the World," *Parabola*, Summer V:3, pp. 14-20.

5. Quoted in Edgar De Bruyne, *The Esthetics of the Middle Ages*, tran. Eileen B. Hennessy (New York: Frederick Ungar Publishing Co., 1969), p. 57.

6. *Ibid.*

7. Plotinus, *The Enneads*, tran. Stephen MacKenna (New

York: Pantheon Books, 1969), p. 109.

8. *Hymns of Divine Love, St. Symeon the New Theologian,* tran. G.A. Maloney (Denville, N.J.: Dimension Books, n.d.), p. 58.

9. Simone Weil, *Waiting for God* (New York: Harper & Row, 1973), p. 105.

10. *Mysticism*, p. 300.

11. Robert Henri, *The Art Spirit* (New York: J.B. Lippincott, 1960), p. 87.

12. *The Praktikos and Chapters on Prayer*, Evagrius Ponticus (Kalamazoo, Mich.: Cistercian Publications, 1981), pp. 33-34.

13. M. Basil Pennington O.C.S.O., *Thomas Merton, Brother Monk: The Quest for True Freedom* (San Francisco: Harper & Row, 1987), pp. 94-95.

14. Pierre Teilhard de Chardin, *Hymn of the Universe* (New York: Harper Torchbooks, 1965), p. 124.

15. Pierre Teilhard de Chardin, *Writings in the Time of War* (New York: Harper & Row, 1968), p. 118.

16. Meister Eckhart: *The Essential Sermons, Commentaries, Treatises, and Defense*, p. 253.

7. The Forest at Night: A Song of Praise

1. *The Collected Poems of Theodore Roethke*, p. 137.

2. *Celtic Christianity*, p. 119.

3. Owen Barfield, *Saving the Appearances: A Study in Idolatry* (New York: Harcourt, Brace and World, n.d.), p. 164.

4. Nikos Kazantakis, *Report to Greco*, tran. P.A. Bien (New York: Bantam Books, 1966), p. 446.

5. *The Hidden Ground of Love: The Letters of Thomas Merton on Religious Experience and Social Concerns*, ed. William H. Shannon (New York: Farrar, Straus and Giroux, 1985), p. 564.

6. *Genesis: A Bible Commentary for Teaching and Preaching*, p. 28.

7. *Man Is Not Alone*, p. 76.

8. *Report to Greco*, p. 446.

9. *Celtic Christianity*, p. 114

10. *God in Search of Man*, p. 46.

11. Thomas Berry, *The Dream of the Earth* (San Francisco: Sierra Club Books, 1988), p. 198.

12. *Report to Greco*, p. 451.

Of Related Interest...

Earth Story, Sacred Story
James Conlon
The author views life as a cosmological whole, and urges
readers to explore the Earth-human relationship in a new
light.

ISBN: 0-89622-583-6, 160 pp, $12.95

Befriending the Earth
*A Theology of Reconciliation Between Humans and
the Earth*
Edited by Anne Lonergan and Stephen Dunn
Thomas Berry and Thomas Clarke dialogue on the role
religion plays in ecological issues.

ISBN: 0-89622-471-6, 168 pp, $7.95

EarthSpirit
*A Handbook for Nurturing an Ecological
Christianity*
Michael Dowd
The author helps readers link basic ecological realities with
the fundamental truths of Christianity.

ISBN: 0-89622-479-1, 128 pp, $7.95

Available at religious bookstores or from
TWENTY-THIRD PUBLICATIONS
P.O. Box 180 • Mystic, CT 06355
1-800-321-0411